T0157201

MORE PRAISE FOR *JESUS, CAREER COUNSELOR*

"Laurie Beth Jones brings light to situations we all confront in our careers. Confused ideas are untangled while you find comfort in her practical teachings."

—Douglas D. Hawthorne, chief executive officer, Texas Health Resources

"Laurie has done it again. In *Jesus, Career Counselor* she shares stimulating insights, solid spirituality, and spot-on-psychology for every-day living all wrapped in the warmth and humor of down-to-earth practicality. She delivers the sizzle and the steak, form and content. A must read for leaders, followers, and those in or facing transition."

—Dick Stenbakken, Ed.D., therapist, retired chaplain (Colonel), U.S. Army, and author

JESUS

Career Counselor

How to Find (and Keep) Your Perfect Work

Laurie Beth Jones

HOWARD BOOKS
A Division of Simon & Schuster, Inc.
New York • Nashville • London • Toronto • Sydney

Published by Howard Books, a division of Simon & Schuster, Inc.
1230 Avenue of the Americas, New York, NY 10020
www.howardpublishing.com

Library of Congress Cataloging-in-Publication Data
Jones, Laurie Beth.
Jesus, career counselor : how to find (and keep) your perfect work / Laurie Beth Jones.
p. cm.
Includes bibliographical references.
1. Vocation—Christianity. 2. Work—Religious aspects—Christianity. 3. Vocational guidance. I. Title.
BV4740.J655 2010
220.8'331702—dc22
2009039522

ISBN 978-1-4767-8637-7

10 9 8 7 6 5 4 3 2 1

HOWARD and colophon are registered trademarks of Simon & Schuster, Inc.

Manufactured in the United States

For information regarding special discounts for bulk purchases, please contact: Simon & Schuster Special Sales at 1-866-506-1949 or business@simonandschuster.com.

The Simon & Schuster Speakers Bureau can bring authors to your live event. For more information or to book an event contact the Simon & Schuster Speakers Bureau at 866-248-3049 or visit our website at www.simonspeakers.com.

Book design by Diane Hobbing of Snap-Haus Graphics

CONTENTS

JESUS

Career Counselor

A NEW VISION FOR YOUR LIFE'S WORK

One day as I walked in a park in Scottsdale, Arizona, I noticed a young man in shorts and a T-shirt wading waist deep in murky water. His head was down, and he moved each foot slowly, diligently searching. Two of his buddies were standing on the shore, chatting and smoking, sometimes calling out encouragement.

I circled the complete park, and when I returned, I asked the friends, "What is he looking for?"

"A hundred-dollar Frisbee," they said. "He's not going home without it."

Today as I took my morning walk, now in Balboa Park in San Diego, I noticed a life-size statue of a woman holding a pinecone in one hand and a garden trowel in the other. This was a monument to Kate Sessions, a horticulturist who planted most of the flowers, trees, and plants in the park over a twenty-year period.

These two images are powerful visuals that depict what this book is about. The first, someone searching waist deep in murky water for a valued treasure. The second, a person holding a treasure in one hand and a digging implement in the other.

Many people do not spend as much time searching for a worthy career as that young man did searching for a Frisbee. He was willing to stop the game he was playing, inconvenience his friends, get into muddy water that was waist deep, and ruin what he was wearing, all to find something that was important to him.

I was enthralled by the statue of the woman in the park because she reminded me that many of us are unaware of the treasure we hold in our hands. And if we simply look, we'll see that we have what we are seeking . . . right there, in our hands, where God has placed it.

If you were a statue with a garden trowel in one hand, what would you be holding in your uplifted palm? What gift has God given you to bestow on the world?

When I asked myself these questions, I imagined that in my hand I was holding a form of pure, life-giving light. I instantly wanted to share it with every person I met. In *Jesus, Career Counselor*, I pray that you will find my words to be life-giving light to you.

If you picked up this book, you are likely dealing with one or more of these questions:

1. How do I choose a meaningful career?
2. How can I reinvigorate the career I currently have?
3. How do I create a new career out of the ashes of an old one?

You very possibly might find yourself in one of these situations. Perhaps . . .

- You've just lost a job.
- You've been wrongly terminated.

- You've been laid off for reasons you don't understand.
- You have an ignorant boss.
- You inherited a family business.
- You want to leave a family business.
- You inherited sudden wealth.
- You suddenly lost wealth.
- You feel different from your coworkers.
- You are being called to relocate.
- You don't want to relocate.
- You don't want to keep doing what you've been doing.
- You feel burned out.
- You are in a fog about the next steps for your career.
- You are trained in one thing but want to do something different.
- You realize you are living out your parents' unlived lives.
- You are just starting out and feel overwhelmed by possibilities.
- You need to learn a new skill set entirely.
- You are feeling irrelevant and passed by in the workplace.
- You feel restless.
- You think there must be something more.

If any of these situations pertain to you right now, this book is for you.

However, this book is more than a manual to help you identify and find the exact job fit. My goal goes beyond helping you decide whether you want to go into pediatrics or neurosurgery, or become a part-time eBay seller or get a job at Home Depot.

These are details to be determined after you have found your *vocare*, your calling.

As we move through the pages of this book, my desire is that your life's work will embody three core principles that I have brought together under the term "spiritreneur." First, *choose work that honors God;* second, *do work that honors your soul;* and third, *earn your living doing the first two.*

Even if you choose to work for a company (and most of us do), you can be a spiritreneur within that organization. To do so, you must understand that you are also working for God, no matter where you are and who your supervisor may be. Thus, like Paul advocated in Colossians 3:23 (KJV), "Whatsoever ye do, do it heartily, as to the LORD, and not unto men."

Jesus, Career Counselor will give you a *new vision* of work that will help you succeed wherever you are and within whatever career you choose—a vision that will help you find, get, and keep work that you love.

A New Vision of Your *Career Path*

God does not necessarily want people to stay in the same job in order to accomplish his purposes. Few roads that lead somewhere grand are smooth—they often climb, wind, and dip. So it is with our careers.

A quick overview of famous biblical characters reveals that the overwhelming majority had uneven careers—and many were either self-employed or worked in a family business.

- *Among the self-employed:* Nathaniel, Samuel, Jonah,

Ezekiel, Isaiah, Elijah, Mordecai, Rahab, Micah, Balaam, Malachi
- *Some who owned or worked in a family business:* Abraham, Noah, Job, Moses, Miriam, Aaron, Saul, Jonathan, David, Solomon, Jacob, Isaac, Laban, Lot, Boaz, Ruth, Peter, Andrew, James, John, Jesus
- *Employees of larger organizations:* Daniel, Nehemiah, Esther, Joshua

Many biblical characters experienced major career transitions:

- Family business to employee: Joseph, Jacob, Moses
- Family business to self-employed: Satan, Adam and Eve
- Self-employed to family business: Rahab
- Employee to self-employed: Nehemiah, Joshua
- Family business to employee to self-employed to employer: King David

In the wonderful book *You Majored in What?* author Katharine Brooks brings chaos theory to bear in career planning. She states that early career planning was founded on the work of 1909-era academic/engineer Frank Parsons, who believed that A plus B should equal C.

She shares, however, that many people—especially liberal arts majors—do not end up working directly in the majors they chose for college. In their cases, A plus B leads to L, which circles back to G and then ends up at R. She shows a revealing graph published by an alumni-association study. A person who majored in physics may end up running a day-care center. A person who majored in English may end up working at NASA. She posits the theory that if we follow the threads of interest in what we are doing and are open to new experiences, we can build an exciting life.

She gives the example of a young woman whose chosen career path was that of professional tennis player via scholarship. However, once in college, this woman realized that she didn't quite have what it took for the tennis grind, and she ended up majoring in English. She then got interested in science. She then got interested in space. She then wrote a letter to NASA. She then became an astronaut. She was Sally Ride, one of the first women in space. How did her lobbing tennis balls lead to shooting for the stars? By following her heart.[1]

You, too, may be on a career path that is winding and dipping and climbing—rather than plodding ahead on level ground. But as you discover more about yourself and the gifts God placed in you, you will see the wisdom in the journey. Hear God's words for you: "Whether you turn to the right or to the left, your ears will hear a voice behind you, saying, 'This is the way; walk in it'" (Isaiah 30:21).

A New Vision of *Work*

There's a misconception around job-getting and work-doing that says they are things we "*have* to do," not "*want* to do." TGIF means Thank God It's Friday, clearly implying that a job is something one is eager to have end or to escape. Where does this thinking come from?

In Genesis we are told that God created male and female to walk with him in a garden and to be fruitful and multiply. As the story unfolds, Adam and Eve disobey God and are cast out of Eden. They are told they are now cursed to work under "the sweat of your brow" (Genesis 3:19). It is no wonder that so many people have come to associate working as a less-than-desirable condition. We seem to forget, however, that the notion of work as a curse was under the law, and that law has been fulfilled for us by the life and love of our Lord, Jesus.

Also in this old story, I see the command to "be fruitful and multiply" (Genesis 1:28 NKJV) not merely in the context of physical reproduction, but in light of what Jesus said in John 15:5 (NKJV), "He who abides in Me, and I in him, bears much fruit." Perhaps we could say that our reconnected state with God in Christ puts us back in the Garden of Eden. Being fruitful means being productive in a beautiful and natural way.

My desire is that you return to your beautiful, productive state . . . where "work" is what you do naturally, like a tree producing fruit or a vine producing grapes . . . where your career is fulfilling and honors God, where it allows you to carry out your mission in the world in flowing and awe-inspiring ways.

A New Vision of *What You Do*

Yesterday I measured a light table for my art studio, taking its height and width and depth. I know from my measurements that it is thirty-six inches high by forty-eight inches wide by sixty-six inches deep. What fascinates me most about this particular table is not its dimensions but the light that comes from within it.

And that is what fascinates me about you. Not your job description, per se—not what you *do,* but what is being poured into the world from your soul while you are working . . . the light that comes from within you.

In Ezekiel 47 we are given a life-changing vision of a man encountering a heavenly being who tells him to measure a stream that is flowing from underneath the temple. As the two continue their dialogue, the stream turns into a river and the river flows into a sea. And all along the river are trees bearing fruit for food and leaves for healing. There are fish of every kind swimming in the river and fishermen making a living on both sides of it. And perhaps most beautiful of all, "Living creatures will live wherever the river flows" (verse 9). I have prayed that my career would be like that. That it would bring life and provide food for thought and healing, as well as support many kinds of fish and fishermen (and women). Wouldn't you want that for yours, too, or for your children?

In order for that to happen, the stream must start under the temple, which is a dedicated place of worship and communion with God.

A New Vision of *Dreaming*

As I consider the workplace, I realize that most of us have two categories of dreams. We either want to *attain* or *achieve.* Almost all self-help books, infomercials, mail-order catalogs, and even wars are dedicated to these two human "dreams." But one day I asked myself, *what might the Holy Spirit dream for us?*

I got out a pen and paper, and these are the words that flowed: to rise, risk, roar, reflect, renew, restore, remain, return, regenerate, revive, release, rejoice. Just like that. Twelve of them. Dreams. Glimmering with mystery and promise. I began eagerly telling my friends and colleagues about what I called "The Twelve Dreams of the Holy Spirit." And as I began to research and explore, I found that these twelve dreams flow through the pages of Scripture. Those dreams became the framework for this book about careers.

I am convinced that Jesus doesn't dream for us a job description. Jesus dreams for us a way of living and being fruitful in the world. He wants us to rise and risk and roar, like the Fire he came to bring. He wants us to reflect, renew, and restore, like the living Water that he is. He wants us to remain, return, and regenerate, like the Earth from which we are formed. And he also wants us to revive, release, and rejoice, like the Wind of the Holy Spirit.

You may recognize the four elements above—Fire, Water, Earth, and Wind—from some of my other books. If not, let me quickly say that I use these terms in books and seminars to define the four different personality types. (For more information, you can read *The Four Elements of Success: A Simple Personality Profile That Will Transform Your Team.*) Simply put—even though each person's personality excels in certain areas and is weaker in others—each of us must have some portion of the four elements in order to live a balanced, productive, dream-fulfilling life:

- Having *Fire* in our hearts allows us to be excited about what we are doing in our careers. The Fire of excitement translates to *leadership skills*.
- We must also have *Water*, so we can bring life to those we touch at work. Water becomes *relationship skills*.
- *Earth* ensures that we are solidly grounded in how we go about our businesses. The earth of grounding translates into *good habits and character traits*.
- Finally, we must be like the *Wind*, releasing our gifts and talents into the world. The Wind becomes the *creativity* and *innovation* that are in high demand in every industry in the world today.

Note: as we move through the book, there will be several places where space is allotted for you to answer specific questions. In addition to that space, there are a few pages in the back of the book you can use however you'd like as you explore the vision God has for you. Let's begin.

Make It Yours

Let's take a quick quiz right now. Read each statement and circle True or False.

FIRE: I am excited to wake up and go to work almost every morning.

True

False

WATER: What I do, or how I do it, brings life, joy, and/or encouragement to others.

True

False

EARTH: I am doing things that will help me succeed.

True

False

WIND: I am actively utilizing my talents at work.

True

False

It could be said that if you lack any one of these elemental constructs in your career, you may never reach the heights God intends for you. But as you adopt the dreams of the Holy Spirit as your own, you will blossom in every area.

A New Vision of *Where to Begin*

As we begin our adventure of fulfilling the Holy Spirit's dreams for you and finding your true vocation, we will lay out four guideposts to serve as markers along your way and help you see the big picture. We'll do this by . . .

1. Exploring your *mission*
2. Assessing your *personality type*
3. Discovering your *four greatest talents*
4. Writing your *vision*

A vocation involves a lifestyle, really. Rather than getting a job and then living life in your leftover time, I believe Jesus, Career Counselor, wants you to build your vocation in all its fullness, with the fulfillment of your mission at its center.

The four sections following are dealt with at length in my previous works, so bear with me while I review them, and forgive lengthy references to further information. This book is really an advanced course built upon these previous works, so I will only dwell on them briefly here.

However, these four points are the foundation for all the material that follows, so take the time to answer the questions now.

1. My Mission Statement

Write out in a single sentence what you came here to do, ideally containing three verbs, and based on one of your core values.

....

....

....

(For more help on this you may go to my website, www.lauriebethjones.com, and click on Books/Shop/Resources from the top menu bar of the home page. From the store landing page, click on "Free Resources" and then on "Free Mission Download.")

2. My Personality Profile

Ask your family and friends which element you are most like: Fire, Water, Wind, or Earth. Write down the answer here:

....

....

....

(In order to determine how much of each element you really are, you may want to click on my website under Path Elements Profile Link, and click on "Take PEP Now." Use the code JCC101 for a 10 percent discount. This download is really worth its weight in gold, as everything you do career wise is impacted by your elemental makeup. You can also learn more in my book *Four Elements of Success.*)

3. My Four Greatest Talents

In the space provided below, draw the image of a medieval shield with four quadrants. (This is your Talent Shield.) Fill each quadrant with a symbol that represents your four greatest gifts. To help you do this, ask yourself: What do people tell me I'm good at? What do I most love to do?

4. My Vision Statement

To help you identify your vision in life, imagine that you have won the lottery, so money is no object. You still want to be working and contributing to society, however, since that is not only what is most healthy for you, but it is also fun. Now imagine it is Monday morning, 9 A.M. What are you doing in your ideal vocation?

....

....

Continue on, by imagining Wednesday at noon. Who are you lunching with, and where?

....

....

It is now Friday evening, 6 P.M. What does your evening look like?

....

....

(For more detailed information on this, please refer to my book, *The Path: Creating Your Mission for Work and Life.*)

Keeping these four guideposts in view at all times will help you fulfill your calling and find satisfaction in your work. Jesus, our ultimate Career Counselor, has his door open and is eager for you to have life, and to live it abundantly.

A New Vision of Thinking—*Meta-Thinking*

Meta-thinking means thinking beyond what you are thinking. According to Wikipedia, meta (from Greek: μετα = "after," "beyond," "with," "adjacent," "self") is a prefix used in English to indicate a concept that is an abstraction from another concept, used to complete or add to the latter. Meta means *after* or *beyond* . . . thinking after your thinking . . . thinking above what you're thinking. *Meta-thinking is thinking about what you are thinking about.*

Jesus constantly challenged us to think about what we are thinking. He asked the woman at the well, "You say you are thirsty, but what are you really thirsty for?" He asked the unemployed, crippled man lying on his mat, "Do you really want to be healed?"

Wouldn't the answers seem obvious? To the common person, yes. But Jesus wants to get to the heart of why we are doing what we are doing, or why we find ourselves wanting certain things.

Meta-thinkers observe things from a higher level. They are able to connect the dots that seem like obstacles when viewed head-on. Meta-thinker Howard Schultz bought a small Seattle coffee shop and turned it into an industry by visualizing a "third place" where people could gather between work and home. Thus, Starbucks was born. Meta-thinkers make sure they not only have the right tools for the job but, more important, that they are doing exciting work in the first place.

I read in Robert Fritz's book, *The Path of Least Resistance*, about a study that looked at the qualities innovators had in common. These innovators had come up with creative, profitable solutions to problems in the workplace.

There were three observable qualities in these meta-thinkers:

1. The ability to tolerate clutter. (Thank you, God.)
2. The ability to simultaneously hold the current reality of "what is" with the vision of "what could be" in their minds as they worked.
3. The ability to see humor in almost everything.

Humor is a form of meta-thinking because it has two layers of focus: one, the observable reality; and two, the humor surrounding it.

Poets are meta-thinkers. Read this:

Pulling out the chair beneath your mind and watching you fall upon God . . . what else is there to do that is any fun in the world?

—Hafiz, interpreted by Daniel Ladinsky,
in *I Heard God Laughing*

These twenty-six words convey a host of meanings about how to interpret "bad news," about how sometimes things that seem like bad news were placed there by a loving spiritual force to cause you to remember your true Source.

In fact, have you heard the term "worth his weight in gold"? That comes from a Persian tradition in medieval times. Back then, poets were treasured and highly valued. They were employed by local princes and provincial governors to create epic verses. When the ruler was especially pleased by a composition, the poet was sometimes placed on a scale and rewarded with "his weight in gold." If you resolve to become a meta-thinker, you, too, will be worth your weight in gold.

There are three types of people in the world.

- Reactors
- Thinkers
- Meta-thinkers

Reactors are, as expected, people who react to situations. I lost a job. Now I need to get a job. Look for a job. Or go to school because my parents said so. After school, still unsure of a career choice, I go back to school. I stay in school as long as possible to avoid real-world scenarios.

Thinkers are people who put some reflection time and thought into their careers. I'm thinking about going back to school. I think I will listen to what Ed/Ted/Fred/Oprah said.

Meta-thinkers ask themselves: What did I come here to do? How and where can I best use my God-given talents?

A New Vision of Your *Calling*

Vocare . . . a Latin term from which we get the word *vocation.* It means "to call or name; to invoke," and *vocation* denotes, specifically, a calling from God. It complements the concept of being fruitful and multiplying and bringing life to others with everything you do. How shall we find our vocations? In the classifieds? I don't think so. We find our vocations by understanding that we were sent here by God with a glorious purpose in mind and that our challenge is to discover it and fulfill it, no matter who we are, where we are, or how old we are.

Ten Questions to Help You Find Your Vocation

1. Are you doing what you most love to do?
2. Are you doing the work that only you can do?
3. Would you do this work even if you weren't being paid to do it?
4. When you are doing this work, do you sometimes get so engaged in it that you lose track of time?
5. Does this work allow you to have the lifestyle that nourishes your soul?

6. Does this work honor God?
7. Does this work honor you?
8. Do you feel like you are pulling someone else's plow? Is that all right with you, or would you prefer to pull your own?
9. Does this work allow you to utilize all your greatest talents?
10. At the end of this work, do you think you will hear the words, "Well done, good and faithful servant"?

I am writing much of this book at a resort property in La Jolla, California. It offers an incredible view of the ocean, distant mountains, and rolling waves . . . all overlooking Spanish tiled roofs below. As I entered the lobby this morning, I noticed two large matching sculptures on a mirrored table. The figures are half-horse, half-fish. I chuckled as I walked past them. *This is exactly how I feel, Lord, about the work I do. Sometimes I am the horse, climbing mountains, pawing at the valley, snorting and whinnying for others to come play with me. And sometimes I am the fish, swimming along in a rolling ocean, flitting through the seaweed, trying to dodge the sharks.*

In today's workworld, many jobs are like those sculptures—half of one thing and half of something else. Your work will be, most likely, a creature unlike any other, as you creatively go about handling a variety of tasks and projects. According to the U.S. Department of Labor, the average thirty-eight-year-old will have held between ten to fourteen different jobs. This is why knowing your calling and the direction God wants you to go is so important.

While here, I see people in jobs all around me. There is the concierge, who seems not to have read her job description. She sits huddled at her desk, reading the paper, head down, avoiding eye contact with everyone. She rarely smiles, and she acts as if anyone with a question is interrupting her. She is an ill-placed, unhappy employee.

Then there is Georgi, my server for breakfast today. His quick smile and flashing eyes indicate to me that he has more intelligence than his job requires. An immigrant from Bulgaria, he takes a daily interest in the progress of my work. He tells me he was an engineer in his homeland but is unable to get a license here. He is a happy employee, working beneath his capabilities.

Across the room from me sits a frowning, gray-haired man in a business suit, talking too loudly on his cell phone. "Of course, Lucas, you will be assigned to the project. Have I ever lied to you?" Long pause. "Listen, I'm telling you, you are my man for this. I wouldn't have it any other way." Click. Next call. "What do you mean Elsa called in sick again? Is there anyone else who can get that data to us within the hour? This is unacceptable!" Click. He is an unhappy employer.

Perhaps two of these people have not yet found their *vocare*, their calling, and are simply allowing whatever comes their way to direct them rather than dreaming about what could be.

I believe that God places our calling within our hearts. But sometimes it's hidden or becomes distorted through time and disappointment or misdirection. I am confident, however, that we can all find our calling, our true calling, again (or for the first time!).

The way to choose a meaningful career is to build one around the four guideposts we mentioned earlier—your *mission, per-*

sonality profile, vision, and *four greatest talents.* Look back to the answers you wrote on pages 12–14. Use meta-thinking to project these into what your next steps might be.

Finding and living your career calling is a journey. It is not a superhighway laid out like a track. What would be the mystery, the fun, the divinity in that?

I have too often seen the tears of people who were channeled and funneled and tunneled into work they were good at but ultimately came to despise. My mother was a very good bookkeeper who yearned to be an artist, and my father was a very competent coffee salesman who yearned to be a social worker. They somehow managed to fulfill their job descriptions yet were frustrated in the workplace, and unable to live out their highest gifting.

When Jesus came up out of the muddy water of the Jordan, the clouds broke open and he heard, "You are my Son, whom I love; with you I am well pleased" (Luke 3:22). To me, this is the be-all and end-all of any good career counseling. As God loved and claimed his beloved Son, he loves and claims each of us as his special creation. We have been given a divine connection with our Creator, and in that connection we can find ultimate fulfillment.

Just yesterday I squeezed into my seat on Southwest Airlines, offered my seatmates some of my trail mix, and then I settled in to pecking away at this book. As we were about to land, the woman sitting next to me asked if I were working on a book. I said yes and told her what it was, and suddenly her face flashed in recognition. She began to squeal in delight, sharing that *Jesus*

CEO had helped shape her career. Now she works in prison ministries in Dallas, along with being an engineer at Raytheon. She is also caring full-time for her mother with dementia, who was wearing pink gloves and sitting quietly beside her. "Thank you for your work!" she said as she hugged me. "Wait till I tell the women in prison that I met you."

As my new friend talked, I had the distinct feeling that she was a better person than I—pouring herself lovingly and willingly into people whom I would probably rather ignore. Yet, somehow, by my finding and living my calling, the words that I delight to write found a way to encourage her on her journey.

It relieves me greatly that, like Mother Teresa once said, I am not called to be great, but to be obedient. When we do that—as we live out our calling—our work can create positive ripples far beyond what we can see.

As you dig deeper into discovering your calling, refer back to your Talent Shield as a filter to help discern which work opportunities will really suit you. When I choose between opportunities, my aim is a 100 percent match.

Make It Yours

Refer to your Talent Shield. In making a job or career choice, ask yourself this question: How many of my four greatest talents will I be allowed to express at this job or in this specific position or in this career?

The goal is to have a match for all four—100 percent compatibility factor. The sad truth is, most of us settle for a 25 percent match, or even less. Does this honor God? It certainly doesn't honor you. Jesus, Career Counselor, does not want you laboring in a job that only uses your lesser gifts. He wants you on his dream team, using 100 percent of the unique talents our God gave you.

Once you understand your mission and what you came to do on this planet, you will never be out of work, even if you do lose your job. A job is a temporary means of delivering your mission to the world. Your mission is always larger than a job.

* * *

Did you know that Joyce Meyers, one of the most successful televangelist/teachers of modern time, was a secretary until the age of forty-two? I wish I could have been a fly on the wall, watching her transition. I have no doubt that she did her work even then as "unto the Lord," but what an ill-suited job that must have been for her God-given gifts. Fortunately, she and the Lord worked it out, and now she fills stadiums with people eager to hear her humorous and "real" observations about life in the Lord.

The artist Georgia O'Keeffe was once asked the secret to success. She said, "Work very, very hard in the right direction." This schoolteacher in Canyon, Texas, might never have become famous had she not encountered a man in New York named Alfred Stieglitz, who became her promoter, champion, husband, great love, and perpetual thorn in her side.

How do you find what that right direction is? There are tests and counselors and, hopefully, friends and family who will help you. Read more books, travel more places, and meet more people, especially Jesus.

Your Career Counselor is calling you. “Come down from that rickety ladder you think is a tree,” he says with a smile, “and let’s have dinner tonight. Let’s break bread, drink some wine, tell stories, laugh, and maybe even cry together. When we are finished, I will ask you, *‘Who do you think I am?’* And in that conversation, you will find who I created you to be.”

PART I

Leadership
Fire

I have come to bring fire.

LUKE 12:49

Fire personality types seek focus and control.
They are quick to act and take center stage.
They bring light, warmth, and encouragement.
They exist to purify and refine whatever is before them.
Fires are bold, assertive, risk-taking, and daring.
They are results-oriented, visionary, and confident.
They are decisive, initiating, and competitive.
They desire to control the agenda, make decisions, and confront obstacles head-on.
The God who created fire wants you to rise, risk, and roar.

CHAPTER ONE

RISE

rise 1 a: to assume an upright position especially from lying, kneeling, or sitting **b:** to get up from sleep or from one's bed **2:** to return from death **3:** to appear above the horizon <the sun *rises* at six> **4:** to extend above other objects <mountain peaks *rose* to the west> **5:** to exert oneself to meet a challenge <*rise* to the occasion> **synonyms:** see *spring*

The word *rise* is used more than 164 times in the Bible. It is the foundational premise of Christianity. It is the essence of everything Jesus says, teaches, and does. (It is also considered a *feminine* word form in the original Hebrew.) And yet, do we rise? Sure, we may get up in the morning and begin trudging through our days, but do we truly rise, into our fullness, our magnificence, our glory?

I will never forget the spring day I watched my three-day-old sorrel filly, Little Pistol, lying in the grass. Her shell-shaped nostrils were flaring in and out as her baby fluff mane caught the morning sun. She had her head resting among dandelions as she stretched out in the warmth of the day. As I stood there watching her out my picture window, something happened.

Suddenly both her little ears flew forward, and I could see her body lift itself up as if by giant puppet strings. She poised for a moment, standing perfectly on point. Then she suddenly leapt into the air and with her feet barely touching the ground began to run full speed around the pasture, kicking out sideways to the left and right, bucking and whinnying . . . fully and suddenly aware of what it meant to be a horse, alive. I tell people: on the first day, she was born . . . but on the third day, she *arose*.

I am wondering if you have yet truly *risen* into your giftedness. Are you aware of the many gifts God created in you, for you to express and enjoy?

Or are you trudging along in your career, unable even to make eye contact with your boss lest he or she notice and fire you?

Are you laboring in a parallel career, one which lets you get close enough to smell the artist's oils and frame her paintings yet can't take up the paintbrush yourself?

Are you laboring in an uninspiring job, thinking that your lot in life is just to make enough to get by?

Then you need a jolt of faith, a spring in your step, because the God of you, in you, says, "Arise!"

To Rise . . . Is to Right What Is Falling

I believe that society consists of seven pillars, which exist to support and challenge the human family. They are:

1. Business
2. Education
3. Health Care
4. Faith and Service Organizations
5. Government
6. Mass Media
7. The Disenfranchised

Study these pillars for a moment. Now, close your eyes and imagine that one of these pillars starts to fall. You rush to help upright it. Which one is it? The one you choose may hold a clue to your *vocare,* your calling. Your work may ultimately touch them all, but chances are you will make your career home in one of these pillars.

If you choose to be a stay-at-home parent, for example, the pillar you are choosing is education. If you choose to be an artist, you are entering the business pillar. This excercise has helped many students, even as young as the seventh grade, to realize that their desires to be rock stars or sports celebrities must be narrowed down into a pillar that serves society in a realistic way. (By the way, the job descriptions for both rock star and sports celebrity are in the business pillar—a fact which adds math as a valuable component of study for even the dreamy-eyed wannabe celebrities.)

There is something innate in life itself that wants to rise. Today in my driveway, for example, I tripped. I turned to find the source of the uneven surface and found it was a root, connected to a tree more than ten feet away. That tree had an innate desire to grow and rise that was so strong it even broke through concrete. It is said that an oak-tree seed exerts the equivalent of three tons of pressure to upend the soil above it.

Boxing enthusiasts go to boxing matches to see not only someone get knocked down but, more important, get back up again, and *rise*.

When Jesus looked at the man lying by the pool of Siloam, he told him, "Rise, take up your bed and walk" (John 5:8 NKJV). This man had been lying by a pool for years, waiting for someone to stir the waters. Yet one word of hope and command by the Lord of creation caused him to suddenly find it within himself to no longer be a victim, but to rise.

Perhaps you are familiar with the image of the phoenix rising from the ashes, a sign of hope and renewal . . . or of Sandro Botticelli's glorious painting *The Birth of Venus*, rising from the sea. You have within you the power right now to rise.

Let's consider some biblical examples and some related concepts of this powerful word.

To Rise . . . Is to Grow

> *The land produced vegetation: plants bearing seed according to their kinds and trees bearing fruit with seed in it according to their kinds. And God saw that it was good.*
>
> —Genesis 1:12

Your work life is indeed a garden, or will be if it is done right.

Make It Yours

Look around you right now, and ask yourself, *What is growing here? What seeds for future positive benefit am I planting? Am I growing? If not, what could I do to grow more?* (Write your answer here.)

To Rise . . . Is to Get Up and Go!

The Lord had said to Abram, "Leave your country, your people and your father's household and go to the land I will show you."

—Genesis 12:1

Perhaps you are being called to go elsewhere. Many of the people who ended up being God's heroes had to relocate, including Moses, Joseph, Abraham, Nehemiah, Paul, and more. The list is long of people whose gifts were needed in different geographical locations.

Is your boss calling you to relocate or transfer?

Is God?

Sometimes indirect transfers are called something else, like being "laid off" or "fired." (For Joseph, it involved kidnapping and prison sentences, so hopefully yours is slightly less traumatic.)

It has been said that "geography is destiny." Look around at your particular geographical location and ask yourself and the Lord, *Is this where I can best serve and use my gifts? Or do I need to look elsewhere?*

I recently read a quote by D. H. Lawrence who moved to New Mexico after a visit to the artist Georgia O'Keeffe. He was transformed by this geographical shift. He said, "When I first saw the sun coming over the horizon in Santa Fe, something stood up in my soul, and I began to pay attention."

Are you being called to a new place, a place in which you can better pay attention to the story of your life? Or are you being called to pay attention to the power and majesty of the geography around you, right now? Sometimes, we live in a place so long, we cease to see the beauty and gifts that surround us.

To Rise . . . Is to "Rise to the Occasion"

Rising to the occasion means that we stand up straight and give our full attention and dignity to the issue at hand. Perhaps there is a confrontation that needs to take place that you have been avoiding. Perhaps, for example, you need to rise up and tell your mother or father that you really don't want to be a ...., but rather a .... If so, please have the courage to rise up and tell them now, despite the shouting you fear may ensue. It could save you and them thousands of dollars and years of heartache.

Perhaps you need to tell your supervisor that you don't want to take on any more projects right now or that you need flextime or that you won't be talked to in that manner again. Some people go to self-defeating extremes just to avoid unpleasant conversations. Don't let an unspoken need or feeling cause you to overreact and leave the whole job, industry, or area, when possibly a "risen" conversation could help alleviate or solve the matter.

To Rise . . . Is to Wake Up

> *Everything exposed by the light becomes visible, for it is light that makes everything visible. This is why it is said: "Wake up, O sleeper, rise from the dead, and Christ will shine on you."*
>
> —Ephesians 5:14

Scripture often implores people to wake up. It is one thing to open your eyes in the morning, and it is something altogether different to truly awaken.

Are you missing something right in front of your eyes?

Do you see the glory in the people around you?

Do you ever just breathe in a moment and say, "Wow. I love the fact that I am here right now, in this place, doing this task, with these people in time"? Are you counting your blessings in your current job, or are you constantly looking for something better in some ill-defined "elsewhere"?

God told Moses to take off his shoes, for he was standing on "holy ground." Where you are standing, right now, is about awakening to the career possibilities and blessings lying right before you. When Jesus said, "Blessed are your eyes because they see" (Matthew 13:16), he was talking to you and me.

To Rise . . . Sometimes Demands a Group Effort

"All rise."

I attended an Anglican church service last week that had me on my feet more than sitting in the pew. It was highly interactive as far as getting up and down, and there was some comfort in being among a group of people who were all clear about what to do together.

Last night I attended a service in a cathedral. I closed my eyes and let my soul be carried as the voices of the congregation rose softly in waves of praise. Tears came to my eyes as people followed the priest's call for all of us to rise—together.

This summer I walked through a park in New York and was amazed to view about two hundred people doing yoga on their lunch hour, all taking various poses and positions at the command of their instructor.

Your career choice, whatever it is, takes place within a group of others. You are part of a community of people who are endeavoring to do something together as a team.

I remember one day being in a building shortly after the September 11 terrorist attack on America. I stood there wondering what it would be like to have the roof of this building collapse on me, as it did for so many workers that day in the Twin Towers. I asked myself, *Would I be proud to have it known that I was here, doing this work, on the last day of my life?* And another question arose: *Would this be the work I wanted to be doing if I knew it was going to be the last day of my life?*

Make It Yours

Picture yourself rising up with your coworkers and your team, or your imagined team, right now. You are all saying something together about your work. What is it? Write it down here.

To Rise . . . Is to Be Elevated Above Natural Circumstances

Do you see someone skilled in their work?
They will serve before kings:
they will not serve before obscure men.

—Proverbs 22:29

If we are in the right place, doing the things we are meant to do, our work will allow us to *rise*. One of the most amazing videos about someone rising into their gifts can be seen on YouTube. It is of a young man who obviously lacks a polished stage presence, who somehow made it through the *Britain's Got Talent* tryouts. He stands there, looking like the grocery clerk he is, and the panel of judges cast a dubious look at him and say, "You don't look the part. But go ahead and sing. We will listen."

This young man opens his mouth and out pours musical notes of "Nessun Dorma," a song from a beautiful Italian opera, and he sounds like a tenor who already has a recording contract. Tears come to the judges' eyes, and the audience slowly rises to its feet, in awe and honor of this young man's musical gift . . . nurtured perhaps in his garage . . . kept secret until now.

It is all of our dreams, I think, to somehow be noticed . . . to be summoned into halls of grandeur and power and recognition. Scripture tells of numerous heroes and heroines who were elevated beyond their natural circumstance. Joseph was elevated out of prison into the ranks of serving Pharaoh. Esther was elevated out of the harem to become queen for more than a day. David was elevated out of tossing rocks at coyotes to bring down giants. So much of what the gospel of Jesus represents is this very notion: that we can somehow—in our current, nondescript, low-self-esteem selves—become elevated to reign with him. But that's our goal, of course, to be recognized by the King of kings, to serve alongside him, be his hands and feet. This is what will give us ultimate satisfaction.

If your goal is simply to become powerful, watch your step. Pride will trip you up. If, however, you become elevated because someone noticed you, saw in you the good and great and the potential of something more, be humble and grateful. True power rests in humility and gratitude.

Make It Yours

Are you doing your job with such excellence that others see your gifts and call you out from the crowd? Have you acknowledged those who are mentoring you, or helping you become better at what you do or how you do it? Are you serving faithfully, with or without recognition? Can you continue to do so, knowing that God sees you, where you are, doing your work, in his honor? Write your response here, to these questions:

To Rise . . . Is to Plan and Prepare

Go to the ant, you sluggard;
consider its ways and be wise!
It has no commander,
no overseer or ruler,
yet it stores its provisions in summer
and gathers its food at harvest.

—Proverbs 6:6–8

I once taught a leadership seminar where not one out of forty-five people had brought anything to write with or take notes on. I thought to myself, *No wonder their bosses are frustrated. These people do not prepare!*

Jesus was very big about people being prepared . . . he told the parable about the bridesmaids rising early and getting oil for their lamps so that when the bridegroom came, they would be ready (see Matthew 25:1–10). He wasn't just telling a wedding story—he wanted us to be prepared for him, at all times and in all places. (Note that he also did not allow the lazy bridesmaids to come into the party afterward!)

It's true that Jesus was anointed for his mission, but he also prepared for it. He memorized the Torah and knew Scripture so well that when tested in the wilderness he knew just the right words to speak to turn temptation away.

Are you getting to work early or scrambling in late?

Are you showing up at meetings without preparation, research, notes, anything to write on?

Or are you rising early to get the work done, to do the research, to be prepared for whatever question is asked of you?

Your Maker Wants You to *Rise*

Perhaps you have been knocked down—by events or circumstances. Perhaps you are just learning something—a task or a new career. Perhaps you feel like you will always be cornered by your fears or doubts. Perhaps you feel put down by others . . . family members or "friends." Perhaps age or illness, financial failures or lost opportunities have you feeling down. You feel more like a beached whale than a warrior.

I am telling you that it is Christ's desire to see you rise.

Rise up and stand for what is important in your life.

Rise up and gather others around you who want to make a change in the world.

Are you walking around under a cloud of discouragement and despair? It is time to rise and shine.

Have you suffered so many losses at work, in dullness and in paper cuts, that you feel your dignity draining out of you?

Your Maker tells you that you are to rise and shine.

Last night as I was writing, I had on my headphones, listening to my iPod. On came one of my favorite songs by Simon and Garfunkel, with the words "Your time has come to shine, all your dreams are on their way." I wondered who they were writing that song for? Finally, as I stared off into space I got the answer. They were writing it for me. And you.

Listen to this dream of the Holy Spirit, spoken through the prophet Isaiah:

Arise, shine out, for your light has come,
and the glory of Yahweh has risen on you.
Look! Though night still covers the earth

and darkness the peoples,
on you Yahweh is rising
and over you his glory can be seen.
The nations will come to your light
and kings to your dawning brightness.
Lift up your eyes and look around:
all are assembling and coming towards you,
your sons coming from far away
and your daughters being carried on the hip.
At this sight you will grow radiant,
your heart will throb and grow full,
since the riches of the sea will flow to you,
the wealth of the nations come to you; . . .

No more will the sun give you daylight,
nor moonlight shine on you,
but Yahweh will be your everlasting light,
your God will be your splendour.
Your sun will set no more
nor will your moon wane,
for Yahweh will be your everlasting light
and your days of mourning will be over.

—Isaiah 60:1–5, 19–20 (NJB)

Do not live beneath your own dreams, nor God's dreams for you. I say to you, arise!

CAREER EXERCISES

1. Has anyone, besides Jesus, indicated he or she has an eye on you to rise into more responsibility or leadership? Name that person/those people. What do they admire in your work? If you can't name people, why not? (Ask them.)

2. Where in your career do you need to rise? Perhaps you need to:
   - Seek a promotion
   - Apply yourself more to the tasks at hand
   - Add education to your résumé
   - See yourself in a new, higher light
   - Other *(Write it here)*:

3. Identify three things that are keeping you from rising. These might include:
   - Fear of failure
   - Fear of success
   - False, negative self-image
   - Unclear path to the top
   - Unsupportive superior
   - Other *(Write it here)*:

4. Have you ever experienced a moment when, like my little filly mentioned earlier, you suddenly became aware of all your giftedness in just being alive? In being particularly, especially you? If so, when was that? If not, imagine what it would feel like *right now*.

....

....

5. Picture yourself as the crippled man lying by the pool. Jesus walks up to you and says, "Rise, [your name], take up your bed and walk" (John 5:8 NKJV). Will you do it?

....

....

A PRAYER FOR YOU

"I am feeling too heavy to rise—anywhere."

Dear Lord, in prayer and meditation I
want to rise with you,
but my cloud never gets off the ground.
Help me shed my inhibitions, my fears,
and the heaviness of my low self-esteem.
Help me take my rightful place
as an heir to the throne,
and rise! Amen.

CHAPTER TWO

RISK

risk 1: possibility of loss or injury: **peril 2:** someone or something that creates or suggests a hazard **4:** the chance that an investment (as a stock or commodity) will lose value

Without the concept of *risk*, most of Scripture would be a boring snore. There would be no journey . . . no battles, no giants like Goliath to slay or chariot chases to outrun, no deep seas to cross, no evil rulers to flee, and no tables to be overturned in the corrupted court of the temple.

From the very first person who said, "I will," to the very last person who says, "I do," the undercurrent throughout the Bible tells us, "You must risk to get the reward." Abram gets a name change and a fortune because of his willingness to follow an unseen God. Esther gets a festival created for her after she breaks the number one rule of the palace in order to advance her cause. (Well-behaved women rarely make history, as the saying goes.)

If he had refused the risk, John the Baptist would not have confronted Herod. Elijah would have ignored Jezebel, even though she had the power to kill him and tried to do so. Peter would not have believed the dream that went against two thousand years of teaching and tradition and that opened up God's favor to the Gentiles. Jesus might not have ventured away from his parents in the temple or sat with scholars far older than he or changed the water to wine or asked strangers to come and follow him.

I could go on and on . . . Mary could have said, "Find someone else to have your child, God." Saul could have kept running down Christians, condemning them to death, rather than writing the words, "Love is patient and kind" . . . and signing with his new name, Paul. And what about the new Christians who were willing to take a risk on Paul, a man who had once killed their own and now wished to lead them?

Risk . . . risk . . . risk . . . risk . . . *Risk* is like *rise* with a kick in it.

Speaking of kick, consider the story of Rahab, who risked her current career status and life to get a better situation for herself and her family (see Joshua 2:1–21). Rahab, the harlot, risked her life and those of her family by helping the Israelites. She (a) negotiated a return of protection for her and her family and then (b) tied the scarlet "signal" cord in the window, confirming their safety and her fate.

Risk is what separates the dreamers from the doers, the wannabes from the victors: Rahab was willing to take a risk. Rahab got what she asked for, what she *risked* for. She is listed in Scripture as someone who had not only the *desire* to act (she was afraid she and her family would be destroyed along with the rest of the city), but also the *willpower* to act (she made a choice to have a chance at a more desirable future).

She was not only *motivated* with excitement and good feelings to do something outside her comfort zone, but also, once she realized she could lose her life doing it, her *volition*, or willpower, kicked in.

From Motivation to Volition

MIT researchers wanted to know what motivated people to change and also why so few "change programs" were ever actually completed in well-meaning organizations. They found that someone can be motivated to do something, yet still not follow through when distractions occur or other things came along.

People who attain great change, or follow through, transcend *motivation* and go into *volition*. They ask themselves, *What will happen if I* don't *do this?*

Make It Yours

Imagine for a moment your situation regarding your career. Have you lost motivation? Your drive is gone. You can't find your mojo to do the same things you used to do. Maybe the question to ask yourself is this: *What will happen if I* don't *do this?* Think about it and write the answer here.

....

....

....

....

Somewhere deep within me right now is a fountain of joy, bubbling up, as all the characters of the Bible begin a new parade. Consider, for a moment, what would've happened if these men and women had *not* answered the call to risk.

Nehemiah would have still been pouring wine, trying not to spill it on the king's Persian rug. But instead, he asked the king if he could return home. The walls of Jerusalem would never have been built without this four-letter word, *risk*.

I see Moses overcoming his stutter to speak to Pharaoh after returning to the land where he was a wanted criminal . . . to rescue the slaves.

I see Joshua returning triumphant, holding the grapes in his hand, shouting, "It is a good land, and we can take it," risking his life in order to bring good news.

King David would have still been herding sheep, rather than taking on a giant named Goliath. Jonathan would never have known his great friend, King David, if he had not opened up to a stranger.

Deborah, the ruling judge in Israel, would have stayed in the "courtroom" rather than venturing out into the field of battle. Mary Magdalene might never have experienced the finest days of her life here on earth, or in eternity, if she hadn't risked trusting Jesus.

This great parade of heroes keep witness to the power of volition.

Life Demands Multiple Risks . . . Even a Kind of Death

Moses had just come off the mountain and delivered the Ten Commandments. His people were obviously in shock and awe that he returned at all, let alone that he spoke to God and lived. How did they respond? "Today we have seen that a man can live even if God speaks with him. But now, why should we die? This great fire will consume us, and we will die if we hear the voice of the LORD our God any longer" (Deuteronomy 5:24–25).

If you had been among the throngs at the foot of Mount Sinai, wouldn't you ask if you could speak directly to God, too? Wouldn't you want to be the next one up the mountain?

But no, not this group. They immediately distanced themselves from the possibility of one-on-one time with the Divine by saying, "You become the mediator, Moses. If we go on listening to the voice of God ourselves, we might be devoured."

Someone told me one time that the two most frightening words in the English language are *God's will.* Do we, like the people surrounding Moses at the bottom of Mount Sinai, believe that if we really listen to the will of God for ourselves, we will be devoured?

There is a kind of "death" we must accept. Jesus said you can't put old wine in new wineskins. He said you must be willing to die to yourself. He said you must take up your cross and follow him. But he also said, "My yoke is easy, and my burden is light" and "Follow me, and I will make you fishers of men."

When we see Jesus at the Mount of Transfiguration, the Bible says he became transfigured. There he was, out on a glorious day, on a mountaintop, having a picnic with his closest friends, and he got so divinely excited that he became transparent.

This was Jesus at work; remember—he was fulfilling the calling his Father had given him. He had died to the confines of the family business and laid down his hammer. He'd risked and embraced a new career of healing, teaching, and preaching; and he ended up on the mountain, hanging out with Moses and Elijah and hearing from his Father, "This is my Son, whom I love" (Matthew 17:5).

When you risk walking into the unknown that God is calling you to, you will potentially encounter your own transfiguration moments on the mountaintop. You will become changed, from the inside out, for the better. But remember, sometimes we must die to the old in order to experience the new.

Make It Yours

What in your life might *you* need to die to in order to live to a new beginning?

Grasshoppers in Our Own Eyes

I just love Joshua. Here he is talking to the Israelites who have been meandering in the wilderness for *forty years.* "So Joshua said to the Israelites: 'How long will you wait before you begin to take possession of the land that the LORD, the God of your fathers, has given you?'" (Joshua 18:3).

Maybe they were discouraged. They had tried before and failed . . . been knocked down. They had been eye level with grasshoppers so long, they sort of resembled them. Maybe their thoughts of doubt and fear were tumbling around and around. But this account is one of the saddest stories in Scripture: the tribes were willing to settle for less *just before* they reached the Promised Land. "This is good enough," they told the Lord. "We are not willing to leave our comfort zone."

Just Beyond Your Comfort Zone

I saw a sign in a gift shop recently that said, "Everything you ever wanted lies three steps beyond your comfort zone." Not that I can't relate to the Israelites' weariness and fear. I get tired of risking and then falling, risking and then falling. It seems that just when I'm delighting in the sudsy scrubbing of a good cleansing *risk* cycle, the rinse cycle begins again, and I go spinning . . . spinning . . . back down into doubt and despair, scurrying back to anything that promises comfort and peace.

My dog Roo barks at my glass-faced washing machine when it's running. It upsets him to see dirty clothes tumbling 'round and 'round. He knows it isn't right. And it doesn't seem right either that my thoughts should be so wishy-washy and gray.

But suddenly the machine's vibration stops. The buzzer sounds. Everything gets still. I reach in and pull out the clothes. There is a freshness and clean smell that wasn't there before.

What was that soap again I used? Oh—now I see the label.

R-I-S-K. Big letters in bold, bright red.

It gets even old rags brighter than bright.

Risk. Yes, risk. Of this, the Spirit dreams for you.

CAREER EXERCISES

---

1. Where are you being called to take a career risk right now? What is it? What is holding you back?

   ....

   ....

2. When have you risked successfully in the past? List *every time* you can think of, including in your childhood.

3. Who else in your company or industry has taken a similar risk and been successful because of it? What did that risk look like for him or her (even if you have to imagine it)? Do you think that person felt afraid, but did it anyway? Do the laws of gravity apply only to a few or to all? Don't the laws of risk/reward also apply equally to all?

4. Imagine, in detail, what will or might happen if you risk, and succeed. Write down the positive vision here.

What will that success feel like? Own that feeling and that image.

5. Risk isn't so frightening if it is broken down into small steps. Try to strip the fear and emotion from the necessary tasks, and just put them down on a to-do list. For example:

The risk is: *ask my boss for a raise.*

The to-do list might look like this:

- *Get information on salary comparison for my job.*
- *Get information about company performance and my contribution.*
- *Rehearse reasons why I deserve the raise and why it is in my boss's best interest to give it to me.*
- *Schedule appointment with boss.*

To-do lists don't need emotional wrappings. They are just words on paper. Write them down.

My risk: ....

My to-do list:

....

....

....

....

....

A CLOSING PRAYER FOR YOU

"I want to learn how to risk."

Dear Lord, I want to learn how to risk.
Show me that stepping out in faith
is the only dance move I need to know right now.
Help me to do it well. Amen.

CHAPTER THREE

ROAR

roar 1 b: to sing or shout with full force **3 b:** to proceed or rush with great noise or commotion **4 b:** to make a loud noise during inhalation (as that of a horse affected with roaring)

There are many ways to *roar*. Since the word is referenced in Scripture only as the sound of lions and thunder and the occasional voice of God, I have looked for the underlying meaning, convinced that the word holds key principles God wants us to learn. We are obviously called to roar at injustice. To stand silently by while others are harmed is not part of God's mindset. But roaring is about much more than simply making noise—it is a call to take note, awaken, and act.

Roaring About Accomplishments

I have a friend who recently initiated, coordinated, and implemented a program that will save her company about six million dollars a year. When she told me about it, I told her to immediately draft a memo detailing the work she did, the steps she took, and the annualized cost savings to the company, multiplied out over the next ten years. She could include the humble words "glad to be of service" and of course add congratulations to the team, but she needed to *roar* about her terrific accomplishment, in writing, to her boss.

She smiled and said a Spanish phrase that roughly translated means, "That must have been a very big egg that was laid, judging by the alert given by the hen." (Roosters aren't the only ones who can crow.)

Nehemiah did the same thing. Consider this passage, written

presumably by him: "So I purified the priests and the Levites of everything foreign, and assigned them duties, each to his own task. I also made provision for contributions of wood at designated times, and for the firstfruits. Remember me with favor, O my God" (Nehemiah 13:30).

King David was not shy about celebrating his accomplishments out loud. In Psalms 26 he says, "I have led a blameless life; I have trusted in the Lord without wavering" (v. 1).

This cry, this *roar* if you will, is not about boasting, but about confirming the accomplishment of work that was undertaken to honor God.

In the workplace, it is important to remember the value of the work you are doing, not only to stay motivated but also to remind your busy boss that you are on the job, doing worthwhile and worthy tasks.

Roaring Through Body Language

There is another form of roaring that has nothing to do with words but more to do with body language and posture. Actors and actresses are supposed to convey their characters not only through dialogue but, especially, through body language. In one television series I watched a female character emerge over time. She began as someone who walked hesitantly, clutching her sweater nervously around herself when spoken to. Her eyes darted to and fro, her hands were constantly coming up to subconsciously cover her mouth. She didn't walk so much as skitter, as if at any moment some predator might pounce upon her.

Yet over time, as she was given more and more obstacles to overcome, her body language began to change. She began to stand up straight, not slouch. She threw her shoulders back, lifted her chin, and walked into a room as if she owned it. This actress only had a few lines of dialogue at a time, yet it was through her stance that she went from a whimper to a roar.

How often do we hold ourselves like victims, downtrodden and beaten, rather than like the victorious, emboldened heroes and heroines Christ has made us to be? Regardless of what is happening around us, we need to rely more on what has happened already within our hearts. If we are confident that we are God's own, captured by truth and covered by grace, we need to embody that knowledge in everything we do and say—including our stance.

I once overheard a dance instructor tell a student, "When you do the Paso Doble, you have to walk in like you intend to take the whole floor." Sometimes people can hear your roar just by the way you carry yourself—like a king or queen. This understanding will serve you well all along your career path.

Make It Yours

How do you appear as you enter a room? Place the biggest mirror you have at the end of the biggest room of your house. Now pretend you're entering a room for the first time. What does your stance say to those who don't know you? The expression on your face? What do you need to do differently?

My Personal Career Overview

Philis Boultinghouse, my editor, asked me to share a personal career overview in this book. I decided to include it in this chapter for various reasons. One is that, being an equal parts Fire and Wind personality types, I have a tendency to roar when something upsets me. (Unfortunately, this can sometimes happen during matters of little import to God's kingdom, such as when driving in traffic.)

Currently I have a small dragon figurine I found in a consignment store sitting on my desk. She is wearing a pink monk's robe, and is sporting a halo, her little manicured claws folded demurely in prayer. Her creator had a sense of humor about how and when dragons roar, as hopefully God continues to have with me.

It was through a roar that my career really took off.

I would *like* to say that my career history went something like this . . .

My parents and the village elders wisely selected me for the writing profession and nurtured me in it from day one.

I went to Destined to Be a Writer School, where I learned to avoid clichés and the overuse of quotation marks around such word combinations as "legal help, or fresh fruit." Upon graduating from said school, I was immediately handed a contract for the first book I wrote, all while music played in the background.

Sure, there were a few stops along the way, but only for refreshment. Singing bluebirds continue to perch on my shoulder, as twelve small but generally happy men do my bidding every day.

However, this is not what happened at all. In reality . . .

My father wanted me to be a business owner or professional athlete, telling me emphatically one day, "YOU WILL NEVER MAKE A LIVING AS A WRITER!" Since my mother constantly out-worded me at Scrabble, she later laughingly confessed that she didn't see my ability with words until teachers pointed it out to her.

I did declare at the age of ten that I was someday going to be a writer and have a horse ranch. My family thought I was joking. However my parents did move to a place where we could have horses in the backyard. That proved to be hugely nurturing for me, as it gave me unlimited time after school and on weekends to ride and think, as well as shovel manure.

After high school, I attended the University of Texas on academic scholarship, majoring in journalism and communications. My first choice for a major was radio/television/film, but I quickly dropped the class when the male professor predicted that of the five hundred students in class, not one woman would get a job in that profession. I believed him. (Wind personalities tend to trust other people and thus believe what they say.)

The only C I ever got in academics was in a subjective poetry course at the University of Texas at Austin. I roared in protest and then dropped out of college altogether, not wanting to be "impropery influenced by people who had no taste." (Here is where my Fire personality kicked up in a negative way. I do regret not finishing college.)

When I became an ardent Christian at the age of seventeen, I also met my husband, who pledged to support me in becoming a writer someday. That pledge lasted until we married two years later, when he suddenly insisted that I drop all career aspirations and become a stay-at-home mom, while he took the truck, controlled the checkbook, and hung out with his friends.

Fast-forward to predictable marriage troubles, which ended in divorce. He kept the truck. I took temporary jobs to support myself, even collecting cans and bottles in parks to help supplement my income. Friends invited me to visit in Atlanta. While there, a boss took an interest in my desire to own my own business. She helped enroll me in night classes at Georgia State University business school. I attended a few classes that I thought I would need.

After about nine months, I returned home to El Paso, where my father got me a job as a lifeguard at the YMCA. When summer ended, I realized my job was ending, too, so I persuaded the CEO to create a position for me as PR Director. I kept that job for two years and then got hired by the YWCA, which was starting a Women's Resource Center. There I met my future boss and now long-time best friend, Catherine C. Calhoun. She observed me in social work and declared that I was not suited for it, but since I love combining art and words, thought that maybe advertising might be a better fit.

Both of us became highly motivated when we went to meet with a bank president for fund-raising. He met us in his office and said, "Ladies, I forgot that I have a funeral to attend. Why don't you gals go shopping, and then we can meet again some other time." We both looked at each other and determined that we were at least as smart—and quite possibly much smarter—than he was. Why were we working for minimum wage? (Note Roar moment.)

Together we brainstormed new, better-paying careers.

We both wrote our mission statements. Hers was "To identify, nurture, and express genius and beauty," which she embodies to this day. Mine was "To recognize, promote, and inspire divine connection in myself and others." (I would later refer to this mission statement many times at pivotal moments in my career.)

Fast-forward to Atlanta friend Sandra Harrison, visiting and sitting on my porch. I was now running my own ad agency in California. She read my journal musings on Jesus as a CEO and said, "Drop everything you are doing and write this book." My ears perked up a little when she said that, as so far my friends and bosses had been very spot-on with giving advice.

I then noticed that every book on business being written was dominated by war or sports language, while I knew that women were the fastest-growing group of business owners.

Bestselling business book titles at the time were *Looking Out for Number One, Winning Through Intimidation,* and *The Art of War for Executives.*

I got really upset when *The Leadership Secrets of Attila the Hun* became the new national bestseller. It was about a man who raped and pillaged for a living, but was now being heralded as a role model for business.

This was my pivotal Roar moment. I decided that rather than stage protests, I would put my pen to work and offer a reasonable business leadership solution from the Leader I most knew and trusted—Jesus.

I wrote the manuscript with no agent, no publisher, and against all current trends and thinking, quitting my advertising business to do so. I rented a trailer in the desert and lived on credit cards while I contemplated the manuscript.

At a networking event I showed the manuscript to a person who told another who found an agent. Rejection slip after rejection slip poured in. Another agent then heard about it and requested the rights to represent it. I said yes. She repackaged the proposal and physically carried it to New York.

Every religious publisher turned it down. Several secular publishers expressed an interest, and Hyperion, which was owned by Disney, purchased the rights.

Jesus CEO instantly hit the bestseller lists and launched my career. My collected works have now sold more than a million copies and been translated into sixteen foreign languages, something I never foresaw in detail when I went out into the desert to follow my call.

I *roared,* and God answered.

I trust that you, too, will figure out a way to harness your gifts and roar.

Make It Yours

Is something happening in your office, company, or community that needs to change? Something that has bothered you for some time, chafing at your soul, because you know it is incorrect or indecent? If so, write it down here:

....

....

....

Sometimes the Holy Spirit uses such "chafing moments" to encourage us to roar. Now write down one way you could make a move to begin to correct this wrong. You can do it! Roar!

I will roar by:

....

....

....

Roaring Demands We Open Our Mouths

This principle is especially important for women, because for thousands of years we have been intimidated and frightened into silence. We were not given the roar power of voting in this country until 1920. I once had a promoter of motivational speakers tell me that women didn't want to hear other women speak, that they would only come out to hear men. I was frankly stunned into silence at his stupidity, so I guess in that instance, his plan worked.

In Song of Solomon the Lover says, "Let me hear your voice" (2:14 NKJV). Only a female soprano can shatter glass with a high C. It is within our power, our purview, our privilege, and it is our *responsibility* not only to speak up but also to roar.

Roaring as a Call to Battle

Deborah is famous in the Bible because she knew how to roar. One of the oldest pieces of poetry in the Bible, the Song of Deborah, was composed shortly after the events it describes. It is a victory song, set in the framework of a hymn, that celebrates the actions of those Israelites who rallied to the call. Of the ten tribes mentioned in the entire song, only four responded. But the point is, if she hadn't roared, *no* tribe would have come to defend the land of Israel.

I have excerpted my favorite parts of the song here. Read it through once for the sheer poetry of it, and then we will go back and look at the relevance of the story to our present times. Notice that all the people mentioned were living out their careers when the battle cry came: Deborah, as a judge, and the others as keepers of sheep or ships, etc.

In the days of Shamgar son of Anath,
in the days of Jael,
there were no more caravans;
those who went forth on their travels
took their way along by-paths.

The villages in Israel were no more,
they were no more
until you arose, O Deborah,
until you arose, mother of Israel!

They were choosing new gods
when war was at the gates.
Was there one shield, one spear to be found
among the forty thousand men in Israel? . . .

Awake, awake, Deborah!
Awake, awake, declaim a song!
Take heart, to your feet, Barak,
capture your captors, son of Abinoam!

Then Israel marched down to the gates;
like champions, Yahweh's people marched down to fight for him! . . .

In the clans of Reuben
there was much searching of heart.
Why did you stay among the sheepfolds,
listening for the whistle, with the flocks?
(In the clans of Reuben,
there was much searching of heart.)

Gilead stayed on the other side of the Jordan,
and why should Dan have stayed aboard ship?
Asher remained beside the sea,
peacefully living with his ports.

Zebulum is a people who have braved death,
Napthtali too, on the high ground of the country. . . .

The horses' hooves then hammer the ground:
galloping, galloping go his steeds.

—Judges 5:6–8, 12–13, 16–18, 22 (NJB)

Let's look at this poetic scene more closely. Deborah, judge/career woman, looked around and noticed that things in the workplace were not as they should be. How did she determine that? Because "there were no more caravans." Trade had slowed to a halt because "those who went forth on their travels" now "took their way along by-paths." People were tiptoeing around the elephant in the living room, as they say. They were going out of their way to avoid confronting the fact that the old path was dangerous. Yet they chose to go around it, quietly, rather than try to fight it or correct the situation.

"They were choosing new gods when war was at the gates." This line is so powerful and so true. Suddenly, when danger appears, who and what people *really* worship is revealed. Deborah perceived people scrambling to take cover and trying to find shelter under other gods' false promises.

In amazement, she looked around and did some math. What did she see? Not one shield, not one spear was found among forty thousand men in Israel!

A woman looks around at the situation in her career workplace or community and thinks, *Surely, someone is going to rise up and take care of this!* She waits, and she waits . . . and then she wakes up and *roars*! She roars and rallies the troops to fight and then moves with those who choose to roar alongside her.

But there were those in Deborah's time who were afraid to take a risk: "In the clans of Reuben there was much searching of heart." They thought about it. They probably even *prayed* about it. Yet in the end, they stayed "among the sheepfolds, listening for the whistle, with the flocks." The verse is repeated again, this time in parentheses for emphasis. "In the clans of Reuben, there was much searching of heart."

I wish I had a nickel for every person who says he is praying about a decision . . . and praying about it . . . and seeking the Lord about it . . . and waiting for God's timing . . . and not wanting to get ahead of the Lord about it . . . and meanwhile the *Enemy* rages, and lives are lost and destinies discarded . . . all while the "clans of Reuben" searched their hearts and waited for the whistle!

Do not confuse "patience" with "cowardice." Patience implies the steadfast faith and knowledge that what you seek will come to pass. Cowardice is shrinking back in fear of an unknown future, seeing yourself as unable to meet the task.

What would have happened if Deborah had not roared? Deborah, career woman/judge, had a lot on her plate. She could've looked the other way, ignored the enemy at her gates. But she had the courage to assess the situation correctly and rally others to do the right thing.

Roaring as a Group Adventure

What will happen in your home, workplace, or community if you do not roar? And who do you need to roar with you? There is much to be said about getting people to agree with you on things that deserve to be roared about. Jesus also spoke of that when he said that where two or more are gathered, "I am there in the midst of them" (Matthew 18:20 NKJV). He also said that whatever you loose on earth will be loosed in heaven. Prayers can become protests, and often need to be.

In Joshua 6, Joshua and his people were able to bring down the walls of a city, simply by roaring together! "Joshua commanded the people, 'Shout! For the LORD has given you the city!'" (Joshua 6:16). What "city" is God promising you, if you can find the courage to gather your people together to shout as one? Think about how collective roaring brings people together, preserves community, and strengthens foundations. Frankly, roaring can be fun.

When a noted civil-rights worker and freedom fighter was about to receive an award, messengers were sent to him as he lay on his deathbed. They wanted to hear from him directly about the hardship, the courage, the many obstacles and death threats he had overcome. So they asked him, "What would you like to say to the people listening to your life story?"

He raised up on his bed and said, "Tell them how much fun it was!"

What would the Bible, your country, your community, your company be like if the people before you hadn't roared? What will your life be, after all, if you die with the roar still in you, faded to a whimper, a whine? Don't let God's call on your heart go unanswered.

Jesus, Career Counselor, wants you to *roar*.

CAREER EXERCISES

---

1. Where in your career are you feeling a need to roar right now? Is it a roar of frustration? Stress? Pent-up anger? A call to action?

2. If you were to picture yourself standing over a defeated "enemy" in triumph *roaring*, what would that enemy look like? Not "who" but "what?" For example, I know a woman who was motivated to overcome the stereotype that "girls are dumber than boys." She worked hard in school and says she felt like roaring when she took the stand as valedictorian of her high school graduating class, with the highest grade point average

of all. She didn't roar "over" anyone, but she defeated a stereotype. What is your particular picture?

3. In the story of Deborah, do you feel like the tribe of Reuben, in whom "there was much searching of heart" yet no action? They never heard the roar of battle . . . only the whistle of sheep calls. Can you roar in response? Why or why not?

4. Where in your past have you failed to roar and regretted it? Was there a time when you tiptoed around, avoiding a critical conversation with your boss, your coworkers, or colleagues? What might the difference have been if you had trusted your instincts and roared?

5. Who in your chosen or contemplated career field is roaring right now and with what result? Are you called to join him or her?

A PRAYER FOR YOU

"I want to find my voice so that I might roar."

Dear Lord, too often I am silent
when I need to speak up.
You gave me a powerful voice for a reason.
Help me know how, and when, to roar! Amen.

LEADERSHIP/FIRE BONUS FEATURES

Prayers for Specific Career Concerns

"I've been fired, Lord."

Bam. The door slammed in my face. The hammer came down. Without mercy, without just cause, perhaps, I have been told I am no longer wanted or welcome at my former place of employment.
Wow, Lord, this hurts. Let me get through any upset, rage, and anger I am feeling. Let me recoil and recover like a spring from this blow, for just as you never answered back to your accusers, I want to model calm and poise and confidence in this public humiliation.
Where I need improvement, either in job skills or people skills, please give me the humility and hunger to improve myself. If I need improvement in my communication style, my ability to think

and act strategically, please send me a teacher, mentor, or coach to help me get better. Even the best athletes do not win every game, score every point, get applauded daily. Help me take this new information in stride, dust myself off, and continue toward my destiny. Help me remind myself that being fired puts me in good company, alongside young David (fired by Saul) and Jesus (fired by the Pharisees). Help me remember that you are my one true Boss, the only one I serve, the only one who can give me the discipline I need to improve and the faith to grasp my next assignment. I love, honor, and bless you. Amen and amen.

"I want to start my own business."

Lord, you know the statistics everyone throws at me when I talk about this. About the high failure rate out there. About how hard it is. And yet in my heart I just have a desire to be my own boss, do my own thing, improve on what I see being done out there. Ignite the flame of entrepreneurship in me so that I do not bury my talents in a dead-end job but go out into the marketplace and multiply.

Reveal to me wise counselors to advise me along the path, acknowledging that it is fraught with dangers and that many are called but few succeed. I have a plan in my heart. Help me put it on paper, test it against the experts, gather wise counsel, and begin. Walk with me as I set out on this path, and I certainly would appreciate any ideas that you have. I am open. I am willing. I am on fire with excitement. Guide me into truth in all things, in all ways. Amen and amen.

Potential Leadership/Fire Occupations

Every personality type needs to rise, risk, and roar, but Fire personality types will especially thrive where they are allowed to use their leadership skills in industries such as these:

- Banking
- Corrections
- Environment
- Restaurant Management
- Sports Management
- Entrepreneur
- Consultant
- Politics
- Athletics
- Project Engineers
- Systems Design
- Finance

- Real Estate
- Urban Planning
- Manufacturing
- Energy
- Health Care
- Education
- Religion
- Government
- Non Profits

Summary Points

RISE: Get up off your pallet of fears and excuses, and rise into the fullness of your creation.

RISK: All the great biblical heroes and heroines took great career risks in order to please God. Will You?

ROAR: God is eager to hear your voice, and the world is waiting for what you know you need to say.

PART II

Relationship Skills
Water

Where the river flows, everything will live.

EZEKIEL 47:9

Water personality types go with the flow and take
the shape of whatever is placed before them.
They take on the toxins and the tears of others—
always seeking order and calm.
Waters tend to be steady, satisfied, and team
oriented.
They are loyal, supportive, and sensitive.
Waters are cooperative, consistent, and trusting.
They desire harmony, the ability to be patient, and
stability.
The God who created water wants you to reflect,
renew, and restore.

CHAPTER FOUR

REFLECT

reflect 4: to give back or exhibit as an image, likeness, or outline: **mirror** <the clouds were *reflected* in the water> **5:** to bring or cast as a result <his attitude *reflects* little credit on his judgment> **6:** to make manifest or apparent: **show** <the painting *reflects* his artistic vision> <the pulse *reflects* the condition of the heart>

Be still, and know that I am God," whispers the water, as you stare into its reflection. Even in difficult times, we are called to reflect on God's glory. Reflection implies a period of time spent, looking, studying, being quiet, thinking. It often implies waiting—sometimes only for a short while—in an effort to hear from God or gather what we seek. Reflection as a work concept has proven to be very profitable. Fifty percent of all new products created at Google emerge from the 20 percent reflection time each employee is offered every month to think about what they want to persue within the company.

I read recently that a world traveler with more than 500,000 miles a year in airline miles has learned to take a harmonica with him everywhere he goes. Instead of fretting about his waiting time in airports, he masters another tune.

Make It Yours

When we wait upon the Lord, we are reflecting on his power and glory. As I scrolled through the word list of *wait* at BibleGateway.com, I was amazed at how many times and ways we are told to wait on the Lord, and the rewards that can come from just being still. Circle every instance of the word *wait* in the scriptures below, and consider what each one tells you about reflection and waiting.

- The LORD is my portion; therefore I will wait for him."

—Lamentations 3:24

- In the morning, O LORD, you hear my voice; in the morning I lay my requests before you and wait in expectation." —Psalm 5:3
- Be still before the LORD and wait patiently for him; do not fret when others succeed in their ways, when they carry out their wicked schemes." —Psalm 37:7
- Yes, LORD, walking in the way of your laws, we wait for you; your name and renown are the desire of our hearts." —Isaiah 26:8
- Since ancient times no one has heard, no ear has perceived, no eye has seen any God besides you, who acts on behalf of those who wait for him." —Isaiah 64:4
- As for me, I watch in hope for the LORD, I wait for God my Savior; my God will hear me." —Micah 7:7
- After waiting patiently, Abraham received what was promised." —Hebrews 6:15

When we wait patiently, we allow ourselves time to reflect on things. When we wait, let us reflect on the goodness of God to us in the past . . . on the gift of wisdom itself.

The Wisdom of Solomon

Solomon loved to reflect on things. While his father, King David, seemed always to be in battle, Solomon loved to think about things, and think about them deeply. It is said he sought Wisdom and yearned for her to be his bride. "And so I prayed, and understanding was given me; I entreated, and the spirit of Wisdom came to me. I esteemed her more than scepters and thrones.

Compared with her, I held riches as nothing." He continues, "And now I understand everything, hidden and visible, for Wisdom, the designer of all things, has instructed me" (Wisdom 7:21 NJB).

He didn't gain Wisdom by doing . . . he gained Wisdom by reflection. Listen further to the words he wrote, and what he gained in his reflection: Solomon saw all the following desirable traits in Wisdom. As you read these words (as I do daily), think about what it would be like if you, in your work and life, could demonstrate these characteristics as well.

Within her is a spirit intelligent, holy,
unique, manifold, subtle,
mobile, incisive, unsullied,
lucid, invulnerable, benevolent, shrewd,
irresistible, beneficent, friendly to human beings,
steadfast, dependable, unperturbed,
almighty, all surveying, penetrating all intelligent, pure and most subtle spirits.

For Wisdom is quicker to move than any motion;
she is so pure, she pervades and permeates all things.
She is a breath of the power of God,
pure emanation of the glory of the Almighty;
so nothing impure can find its way into her.
For she is a reflection of the eternal light,
untarnished mirror of God's active power,
and image of his goodness.

Although she is alone, she can do everything;
herself unchanging, she renews the world,
and, generation after generation, passing into holy souls,
she makes them into God's friends and prophets; . . .
Strongly she reaches from one end of the world to the
other
and she governs the whole for its good.

—Wisdom 7:23–30 (NJB)

To reflect on something means to process it . . . to think about it a little deeper . . . to let it ruminate in your mind . . . to seek to make sense of it. And oftentimes, seeking multiple advisers as we reflect brings us the answers we need: "Come now, let us reason together" (Isaiah 1:18) and "Plans fail for lack of counsel, but with many advisors they succeed" (Proverbs 15:22).

We All Need Time Alone to Reflect

Jesus often went off alone to pray. He needed to reflect . . . to pour his heart out; he needed time to let the gentle, silent hand of his Father sort the wheat from the chaff . . . the pain from the gain . . . the good from the bad.

Even King David learned to settle down sometimes. After the din of battle or the dancing in the streets, he drew apart and penned this psalm.

My heart is not proud, O Lord,
my eyes are not haughty;

I do not concern myself with great matters
or things too wonderful for me.
But I have stilled and quieted my soul;
like a weaned child with its mother,
like a weaned child is my soul within me.

O Israel, put your hope in the Lord
both now and forevermore.

—Psalm 131:1–3

I love this particular scripture because the image is one of a sleeping child, resting securely in the arms of his mother. Sometimes we get ourselves too worked up over things that are really not ours to be concerned about. This verse reminds me of this truth.

The Watery Deep

In Genesis 1:2 we read, "Now the earth was formless and empty, darkness was over the surface of the deep, but the Spirit of God was hovering over the waters." One of the best reasons for taking time to reflect is this very verse. At the beginning of Genesis (1:1), we see God at work in all the elements. And in this second verse, we see that even when things were "formless and empty, darkness was over the surface of the deep," the very Spirit of God was moving.

Do we take the time to contemplate that fact, even when we are in despair? Even when our world has lost its shape and form? Even when our world seems empty?

I wrote this chapter on the Pacific Surfliner/Amtrak train, heading up to visit a client outside of Los Angeles. As the train was rocking and racing along, I gazed out the window and saw a string of low-flying birds skimming the water. I'm used to seeing pelicans do this, but these were smaller birds. I quickly began counting them and lost count when I hit fifty-two. There was a break in the line, and as I looked farther up over the water I realized with a gasp that the entire surface was brimming with thousands of these delightful avian messengers—hovering over the face of the deep, showing that God is on the move. Even when we are waiting and not seeing things clearly, forces in heaven can be moving just like these messengers—winging answers to you even as you race along.

Make It Yours

Is God trying to tell you something right now, something you can't discern because you need time, space, or direction? What do you think he is trying to say? Having trouble hearing it? Then:

- Take half an hour away in a secluded place where no one can interrupt you.
- Turn your cell phone off.
- Then take five minutes to clear your mind of all your "to dos." Write them all down on a piece of paper. Now fold it up and set it at least five feet away from you.
- Then pray this prayer: *Father, I am here. I am yours. Cleanse me of thoughts that keep me from you. What is it you want me to know, right now?* (Remain silent for a time.) *What is it you want me to learn?*

(Remain silent for a time.) *What would you like me to do?* (Remain silent for a time.)

- Listen to the urgings of your heart—how God speaks to you. What do you sense he is saying?
- You might get a general response. If so, ask clarifying questions, such as: how? when? why? where?
- And you might only hear silence. Consider that a response of silence is not a punishment but an encouragement in itself. Perhaps the time is not right for you to know what you seek. Perhaps he is asking you to be still . . . to wait awhile longer . . . to trust.

As I read through Scripture, it becomes evident that whenever people hit a major career turning point, they took a moment to reflect. Isaiah, who sees himself a small man from "people of unclean lips" (Isaiah 6:5), is asked to become a prophet and speak words of healing and reconciliation to an entire nation. He reflects on his situation and is then given a healing vision that, once believed, allows him to freely begin his "career." It is also Isaiah who wrote: "In the year that King Uzziah died, I saw the LORD" (Isaiah 6:1).

I have often used this passage to remind people that when the order of things changes, it is then that perhaps we can see more clearly what God has in store for us. Perhaps you could substitute your own situation for Isaiah's, such as: "In the year that [*such and such took place*], I saw the Lord." Sometimes the watery deeps that God calls us to can only come through the liquid healing of tears.

If you are contemplating a career move or career change or a career, period, it is best to begin with *reflection*.

What Do You See in the Mirror?

Another form of reflection is to take a look in the mirror and see what is there. "As water reflects a face, so a man's heart reflects the man" (Proverbs 27:19). Take a good, long look. What do you see in the mirror? Do you like the person you have become? Not regarding outward appearance, which matters not to God, but regarding your inner "core," your soul?

Do you like the "future self" you might see if you pursue the career path you are contemplating? It is a frequently used dramatic device to have the main character pause and stare into a mirror at some point in a play. "Who are you?" asks the reflection in the mirror. "Is this who you wanted to be?"

I remember so painfully several years ago when I was forced to look in the mirror. I was in the business of "flipping houses" and had purchased a home that had rapidly appreciated. The tenants had been unable to make the payments, and I "flipped it" to another investor. My secretary said she had spoken with the tenants and that I might want to go out and meet them.

I did, driving out to a part of town where I wouldn't normally go. I made my way into the house and was met with a young mother in a wheelchair and a small boy who seemed to be autistic. As I was sitting there with the woman, the father came in, after being out looking for another job. He was partially blind. I sat there in their kitchen, with dirty dishes overflowing in the sink and clothes strewn about the floor, and I realized that these people were not deadbeats but a family trying very hard just to make it through the day. I suddenly resolved to stop the sale and help them stay in their home. *The deal is still in escrow,* I thought. *I can cancel it.*

I called the investor who had made the purchase and said I wanted to stop the sale. When I told him about the tenants' plight, he said, "So what. A deal is a deal. If you don't proceed with this sale, I will sue you." The deal went through. Afterward, I took a portion of the proceeds and tried to find the tenants. I wanted to present them with a check that would help them relocate and start over again. But they were gone and had left no forwarding address. I stood in the yard, overgrown with weeds, thinking about profiting from a process that involved a struggling family losing their home. As I stood there in the Arizona heat, sweat trickling down my back, I realized I could not find them to make this right. And suddenly the "mirror" appeared and asked, "Is this the person your Father wanted you to become?"

The reflection was especially harsh that day.

I lost my taste altogether for that business, and have never done it again.

Look in the mirror and ask yourself, "Is this the person my Father wants me to become?" Jesus asked this question daily and made his career choices accordingly.

Make It Yours

Ask yourself, "Am I everything my Father wants me to become? How does he want me to grow/change?" Now write your answer here:

....

....

....

....

....

God Can Do What We Cannot

When you are thinking you cannot do what is being required of you, reflect on the "accomplishments" of God. Take a nature hike and contemplate the intelligence and power of the Creator who indeed created *you*. Take a stroll through Scripture and reflect on the accomplishments of God in history—of creating *your* world, of leading a people out of exile, of healing the sick and raising the dead. This is *your* God: the God who knit you together in your mother's womb, the God who sees you as you really are. You have uninterrupted, unlimited access to this power. How can you ever be afraid again?

Reflect on all the joy that has been granted to you; remember all the blessings that, like oil, have been poured upon your life. As you reflect, seek Wisdom, for she will serve you in every endeavor.

Here are just a few of the ways you can seek God's wisdom:

1. Devour Scripture as it were your very food.
2. Read biographies of others who have overcome difficult circumstances.
3. Pray.
4. Choose friends with whom you can regularly meet to talk things over.
5. Study history. Learn what worked and what didn't.
6. Ask that God give you dreams for clarification or instruction.
7. Write out multiple scenarios titled "What if . . . ?"
8. Attend worship and/or inspirational services or meetings.

9. Read. Read. Read. Read the writings of wise men and women. And then read some more.
10. Walk with Jesus and ask, "What would you do?"

Go to the Well

She went alone to the well in the middle of the city at a time when she knew no one else would be there. She was tired of being mocked and looked at with scorn. She was weary of the whispers. Most of all she was tired of what she had become. And then she saw someone standing there, with a smile. He began to talk to her and ask her questions—not in an accusing tone—but as if he already knew the answer and wanted her to know that he knew. Two people at a well. He saw through the external appearances and circumstances of her life. He looked *into* her, not *at* her.

In the well of his eyes, she slowly noticed her reflection, and as Jesus took her hand, she suddenly saw "beautiful."

Jesus, Career Counselor, wants you, too, to reflect and see "beautiful."

CAREER EXERCISES

1. How much time do you take every day to reflect on who created you, on where you are going, and why?

2. How could you carve out a little more time, space, and silence to listen? And hear? Brainstorm here:

3. If you asked yourself in the mirror, "Is my Father pleased with the work that I have been doing?" What would be the answer?

4. How willing are you to wait, while you reflect, on God to move or respond? If it is difficult, what do you think he wants to teach you in waiting?

A PRAYER FOR YOU

"I can't still my mind enough to reflect."

Creator God, you made me and my busy mind.
Help me to be still.
Still my body, slow my heartbeat, calm me.
Show me how to set aside all the things

that fill my thoughts and interrupt my time
with you.
You are the God who holds the world and time,
as well as my very life in your hands.
Please, Father, help me see you more clearly, in
all of it. Amen.

CHAPTER FIVE

RENEW

renew 1: to make like new: restore to freshness, vigor, or perfection <as we *renew* our strength in sleep> **2:** to make new spiritually: **regenerate 5:** to begin again: **resume 6:** replace, replenish <*renew* water in a tank>

I only had to renew my driver's license; I didn't have to take the driving test all over again. The forces declaring that I needed it renewed weren't saying I couldn't drive, or that I hadn't been driving, but simply that it was time for a checkup, a reminder of the privilege I have been given. This required renewal, which came in the mail and made me remember how much I love driving and that it is a privilege. It also made me want to follow all the rules of driving, so I wouldn't lose my license.

Sometimes my computer goes into overdrive, and the little circle on the screen just keeps spinning and spinning but never comes to a resolution. It is at that point that my technology person tells me to turn it completely off and reboot. But I'm always inclined to ask, "Why would I turn it off when that is the exact opposite of what I want it to be doing, which is working faster and harder?"

Call it the law of physics . . . of nature. Sometimes when you feel you most need things to speed up, God says, "It's time to turn off for a moment and refresh the controls. It's time to stop the spinning and start over again . . . with a clean sheet, a clean desktop, a clean and refreshed mind."

The Power of Sabbath Renewal

I regularly have to remind my clients that even God rested on the seventh day. Studies show that most of us simply do not get enough sleep or rest. People who maintain that they can get by on five or six hours are fooling themselves.

I met with a salesman not too long ago who had been trying for three years to present me with a proposal. (His persistence finally paid off.) He flew in for our meeting, yet when he got there and had my full attention, he could barely keep his eyes open! He had taken a red-eye flight and admitted that his dogs, all three of them, sleep with him and his wife. The dogs are all on different schedules, so he gets up about three or four times a night to let each one of them out. This salesman, who was sleep deprived and thus unfocused did not get the sale he hoped for.

"Remember the Sabbath day by keeping it holy" is not a commandment for God's ego. It is an important part of how we are wired. We need at least seven hours of sleep, and we are only designed to work six days a week. Why not follow the Creator's advice on this?

Racehorses are not supposed to run every available race. One of the main decisions a trainer makes is how and where and how often to run the horses under his or her care. No trainer in his right mind would put a horse into every single race. Yet that is how most of us live our lives, thinking we can continue to perform without rest.

You may say, "Well, if you had my schedule and responsibilities, you would see that I don't have time to rest."

Not true. That is an example of poor boundary setting and poor time management. Here is a list of ten things you can do to help build more rest into your schedule:

Ten Tips to Help You Build Rest into Your Schedule

1. Book meetings with God on the calendar for soul-care time. Treat it as if he were your most important client (because he is).
2. Do as Jesus did and row away from the crowds. You don't always have to be on duty. He wasn't.
3. Listen to worship songs and classical music to restore your soul.
4. Watch a kitten take a nap. Realize how cute you think it is. Realize that God would think it were cute if you took a nap, too.
5. When you need to take a short break, put up a Do Not Disturb sign, and enforce it.
6. Avoid negative news before bedtime. Spend those precious minutes reflecting on your blessings and your intentions for the next day.
7. Take a mental-health day. Don't wait to call in sick. Call in "well."
8. Book your sleep time as a primary health-and-wellness issue, not as a medal for endurance for going without.
9. Ask yourself if you would want your brain surgeon to sleep as little as you do, and then respond accordingly.
10. Imagine that you have already passed on to the next life. I do this frequently, which allows me the perspective to know that things can, could, and will

continue without me. Why not enjoy the life you have now? The rest you can have now?

Couples who want to renew their wedding vows are saying, "We choose each other again." Professionals who renew their certifications and licenses are saying, "We choose to stay in this profession." People who renew friendships make that extra call or apology or trip to demonstrate the importance of that person to them.

Not too long ago, I tried to figure out why one of my longtime friendships had died. My other friend (I do have two) and I cogitated and ruminated over it.

"Do you think it was when *this* happened?" she asked. "No," I said, "I talked to her after that and she seemed fine."

"Do you think it was because *that* happened?"

We went through every possible configuration of why the relationship had died, and then one day it suddenly occurred to me. I got on the phone and called Catherine. "I finally found out why it died," I said.

"What is it?" she asked. (I'm certain she thought my answer was going to be huge.)

"It died because I simply stopped making the effort." The only pulse the so-called friendship had was the one I was injecting into it.

Maybe your current career is like that. The job jumps only when *you* apply the electric paddles to it. It brings no life to *you*. This might work for a little while, but ultimately, even doctors sworn to save lives look up at the clock and call the time of death. The question on the table is, how are you making the effort to renew your relationships or your job? How often? And are they worthy of being renewed, or are they on artificial life support?

If you have a computer like mine, give it a chance to renew itself, or reboot, before you hurl it at the wall. And before you hurl yourself over the cliff, (i.e. quit), take a little time to renew your mind and heart and spirit, and see if things don't look different in the morning.

A Fresh Look at Your Skills

Sometimes the way to go about a career search is to renew your mind-set about your skill set. Recently I met with a young man who was stalled and discouraged in his job search. Having returned from a self-financed six-month trip around the world, he now faced the prospect of applying for work in a shrinking job market and a career that was seeing much of its government funding dry up. He had put in more than one hundred job applications for his degree field all over the United States, with only one job interview surfacing. Unfortunately, the picture was discouraging.

He was thinking about going back to college for a Ph.D. in his field but was unsure of the value of adding on more debt to his existing student loans for a field whose highest salary would not justify the expense. When I sat down with him for an informal discussion, I asked him how he became interested in this field. He said his parents had suggested it one day, and since it only required a two-year, postgraduate master's program, he thought it was a good idea.

I quickly surmised that this affable young man was a Wind/Water personality type. His eyes lit up when he spoke about his friends and travel. I could see that he was not money oriented, living very frugally, so he could afford to travel. I also surmised that his apparent lack of direction was not laziness, as some adults in his circle had accused; rather, his personality type was inclined to go with the flow.

I asked him if he had ever considered teaching. The demand, particularly for math and science teachers, is huge. Plus, he could travel during the summers, have multiple holidays off, and make nearly as much money as he could in his chosen degree field, which was basically drying up. He indicated a high level of interest. We then went online and found multiple job postings in his city of choice. I also asked him what kind of atmosphere he would like to work in. He is a surfer, and his eyes lit up when I mentioned such places as Salk Institute, which is near the ocean. We went online and found multiple job postings there as well. If he got a job at Salk, he would be surrounded by other "cool" coworkers, no doubt, in an award-winning building that overlooks the ocean. He could go surfing after work.

In the interim, we found multiple tutoring positions he could qualify for, including some that paid $125 an hour. After six hours of focused time and conversation and four hours of online research, he had gone from a discouraged man trying to find a job in a very narrow field to a *renewed* man who was excited about a whole new world of career possibilities.

The Right Work Leads to Constant Renewal

You want and deserve to find work that suits you, and nourishes you, just as much as you suit and feed it. Here are some tips to help you renew your mind-set about your skill set and job search:

Ten Tips for a Renewed Job Search

1. *Know your personality.* Don't pretend you want something you don't or let friends or family tell you what you should be doing. Waters and Winds will need more structure and companionship in career searching, not being interested in doing things alone. Fires and Earths will be more intense and methodical in their searching. Your career choice needs to be a match for your personality as well as your skill set and training—not your friend's or family member's.
2. *Never limit a job search to a job description.* You know the cluster of skill sets you have that would apply to multiple fields. For example, I worked with a litigating attorney who wanted to enter the real estate and construction industry among a group of investors. Some of them viewed him as not having the skills required to do the job.

   Yet as we talked, I pointed out to him that his training might have been in law, but as a successful attorney, his skill set was being able to see the merits of both sides of an argument and get people to come to an agreement. This skill set could be an incalculable asset when negotiating deals, no matter what the field. Likewise, a "stay-at-home mom" job description encompasses the skill sets of project management, finance, conflict resolution, transportation routing, and leadership training.

3. *Know your ideal work setting.* The notion of working in a place near the ocean doesn't have to seem farfetched. But you have to know what you're looking for. Do you want to work at home, among others, in a fancy building, in a shopping center, on a ranch? Do you want to be in the audience or on the stage? Work with large groups, in intimate gatherings, or among others? Target your interviews toward your ultimate goal, and know what you are looking for.
4. *Know your ultimate lifestyle goals.* I even considered calling myself a "lifestyle architect" at one point, for that is what good career counseling is. When you get a job or a career or a vocation, you are getting a lifestyle.

   For the young man I worked with, his desired lifestyle was having time to travel and be free, as well as being near the ocean. Teaching science on an "open summer" schedule would allow him to meet his ultimate lifestyle goals, as well as to live in his desired geographic location.
5. *Take temporary work while you figure things out.* Knowing that you are earning money helps alleviate the fears of starving and helps your psyche maintain a necessary baseline of satisfaction while you seek out

your higher goals. It also gets you circulating in the workforce, meeting other people who can help you.

6. *Get a career counselor.* What was it costing the young man I mentioned *not* to have professional help? His parents are both business professionals. Yet they could not help him thread this particular needle of life because that was not their field of expertise. Would you build your own house from scratch? Make your own clothes? Grow your own groceries? Design your own computers? Every day we pay for the expertise of others in a hundred ways. Yet when it comes to the very notion of our own livelihood, we expect to figure it out on our own. It is not so easy. Please do not end up with a CBD (career by default) because you did not want to pay for professional guidance.
7. *Find out what people are wanting and paying for, and then go do it for them.* My friend Rabbi Daniel Lapin writes, in his book *Thou Shalt Prosper*, that the Jewish race has traditionally become successful even in difficult, hostile environments because they look for what the needs in the marketplace are and then go meet them.
8. *Don't ignore the issues.* I saw a quote on a coffee mug in a Santa Fe art gallery that said: "She could easily keep her balance as long as there were no issues surrounding her destination." If you are finding yourself out of balance in your career search, consider that there might be issues surrounding your destination.

Many times our lack of success is actually a lack of clarity about what we really, I mean *really*, want. Are we walking on our path or being drafted onto someone else's? What issues have you not clearly identified that are keeping the destination murky, cloudy, threatening, unsure?

9. *Get out of the house and network.* Go to trade association meetings or Chamber of Commerce functions. Go online and Google local meet-up groups that might have an interest in what you like as a hobby or as a career field. Do not isolate in your search. You need to extend yourself in as many arenas as physically possible.
10. *Find work that allows you to be happy in your own skin.* In one of her recent columns, author Maureen Dowd took a bemused look at France's new first lady, writing "Carla is playing her role well. She is *bien dans sa peau*, happy in her own skin." Your career must ideally offer that same feeling.[2]

Unhappy in Our Own Skin

Nothing robs us of contentment and satisfaction with who we are and what we are doing like *guilt*. Guilt is symptomatic of uncertainty about our identity and the choices we are making, and it keeps us from being *bien dans sa peau*—happy in our own skin.

The two authors who wrote *I Was a Really Good Mom Before I Had Kids*, Trisha Ashworth and Amy Nobile, interviewed more than a hundred mothers about their lives and livelihoods. The one thing they found the mothers all had in common was *guilt*. No matter what these moms were doing, they felt at some level it was not the right or perfect thing. "If I stay at home and home-school them, am I denying them the socialization of a more communal setting?" "If I work outside the home, am I denying them the baked-cookie-smell-from-the-oven when they arrive back from school?" Their dreams of being the "perfect mom" didn't align with their realities. Because they were judging themselves by others' standards, they could not be happy in their own skin.

Renewal of the Spirit

You see, the things we get so accustomed to moaning about or fixing up or storing will all pass away. Everything will become new again: "If anyone is in Christ, he is a new creation; the old has gone, the new has come!" (2 Corinthians 5:17). And all of this will happen in "the twinkling of an eye" (1 Corinthians 15:52)—or with a twinkling of an "I" as I like to say.

To be a new creation means that you begin to see the world through new eyes. You begin to have new appetites—new priorities, new goals in life. Just as heart-transplant recipients sometimes report new cravings (for hamburgers or motorcycles, for example), when you receive God's heart, you will begin to discover truths you never knew.

Make It Yours

How do you gain spiritual renewal? Here are ten ideas to get you started.

1. Pray that God would renew you any way he sees fit.
2. Journal about your desire and what he is saying to you.

3. Schedule time for retreats on your calendar—an hour a week, a day per quarter, a weekend per year.
4. Seek God's wisdom by reading books that encourage you on the renewal track.
5. Recognize the importance of geography—do you want to be washed in the waves of the sea? Brushed by the winds of a mountaintop? Surrounded by the waving wheat of the plains? Go there.
6. Treat renewal as worthwhile and as valuable as gold.
7. Surround yourself with silence.
8. Go on a pilgrimage or walkabout.
9. Give someone your confession. Or write it down and watch it burn in a fireplace. "Then go and sin no more."
10. Seek a spiritual director or coach.

The Promises of Renewal

Your "I" will see differently when you are renewed. There will be no great divides in your psyche, between who you are and who you want to be. There will be no barriers to understanding what God has for you. You will begin to know, even as you are known. You will begin to see, even as you are seen. You will begin to leap for joy, as you see old things pass away and everything made new again.

You, too, will become *bun diem sans peau*, happy in your own skin. Better than any skin cream. Better than any surgery. This renewal thing begins within.

Pay attention to how God is seeking to renew you now.

This is what God the LORD *says—*
he who created the heavens and stretched them out,
who spread out the earth and all that comes out of it,
who gives breath to its people,
and life to those who walk on it:
"I, the LORD, *have called you in righteousness;*
I will take hold of your hand.
I will keep you and will make you
to be a covenant for the people
and a light for the Gentiles,
to open eyes that are blind,
to free captives from prison
and to release from the dungeon those who sit
in darkness. . . .
See, the former things have taken place,
and new things I declare;
before they spring into being
I announce them to you."

—Isaiah 42:5–7, 9

Jesus, Career Counselor, wants to you be renewed.

CAREER EXERCISES

1. Are you getting enough sleep? At least seven to eight hours a night, no matter what? If not, how can you begin to do so?

2. Are you taking at least one full sabbath day a week—where you do no work, no e-mailing, no deal making? God rested after six full days of working. Why not you? How will you preserve the Sabbath and keep it holy?

3. What in your career or job needs to be renewed? Maybe you have lost interest in the work you are doing. Maybe you have lost some of the scales off your protective layer, like a fish swimming too long upstream. Maybe you need your boss or coworkers to take a renewed look at the value you bring. Write down your thoughts here:

A PRAYER FOR YOU

"I'm in need of rest and renewal."

Dear Lord, you alone know how to make
something old feel new again.
I need the kind of deep rest in my soul that King
David spoke about so often.
Polish me. Shine me up. Make me new again.
Amen.

CHAPTER SIX

RESTORE

restore 2: to put or bring back into existence or use **3:** to bring back to or put back into a former or original state: **renew 4:** to put again in possession of something **synonyms:** see *renew*

Restore is such a beautiful word. It implies promise. It means something deeper and more transformative than the word *fix*, for example. It means that time was taken to consider the original condition of something. Craftsmanship was employed to make sure that the parts work with the whole again. It means that which was lost was brought back.

I learned the value of the word *restore* when my mother began having hip problems in her early eighties. Her hip would "go out," causing excruciating pain. The doctor gave her pain medication, which she could not tolerate, and sent her to a physical therapist who did water therapy with her. Her hip would feel better for a while but then would "pop out" again. This cycle continued for about a year. One day my mother discovered a yoga studio in a local strip mall in Sedona.

She went in, and when she talked about her hip pain, the smiling young woman there urged her to take yoga classes. Mom agreed and found that combining yoga with massages really worked for her. Within a year she had thrown away her cane, and her hip has not "gone out" since. The physical therapist could put the hip back into place, but without *restoration* of the muscle tone, there was nothing to hold it there. Yoga was what worked to put her hip back in wonderful working order. (She is now approaching her eighty-eighth year and is attending yoga classes six days a week.)

I include this story because it is typical for many who lose a job to consider themselves broken until they find another job. Finding a new job does not denote true restoration but sometimes a temporary fix. Because whatever is keeping us out of alignment in the job we lost in the first place is going to "pop out" again later—that is, until you are restored to meaningful work conditions and atmosphere, strengthening your "core."

Restoration is an important part of the character of God. We see in the book of Job that even though he lost everything, at the end of the story all is *restored* to him, and more.

I often think of the story of King David who went off to fight a battle, only to return and find that the enemy had stolen his goods and kidnapped his family. David prayed very hard, went off to find them again, and did not rest until his family was restored to him (I Samuel 30:5–18). David understood, however, that there was more than people and goods and lands to restore.

He wanted God to restore his *soul.*

One of the world's favorite psalms, written by David, is Psalm 23.

The Lord is my shepherd, I shall not be in want.
He makes me lie down in green pastures,
he leads me beside quiet waters,
he restores my soul.
He guides me in paths of righteousness
for his name's sake.
Even though I walk

through the valley of the shadow of death,
I will fear no evil,
for you are with me;
your rod and your staff,
they comfort me.

You prepare a table before me
in the presence of my enemies.
You anoint my head with oil;
my cup overflows.
Surely goodness and love will follow me
all the days of my life,
and I will dwell in the house of the LORD
forever.

—Psalm 23:1–6

We are such a driven society when it comes to work that most of us *really* need to take a time out and restore our souls. Notice how the Lord did this for David. He took him out to a green pasture and led him by quiet waters. He took him out of the city and into the lush countryside.

Water is such a restorative element. It would be well for us if we all spent more time in water, around water, staring at water, drinking more water, listening to water, walking by water, getting close to water. After I encountered deep financial losses in the real estate deserts of Phoenix, I deliberately decided to go to the sea, and I spent hours simply contemplating the constancy of the waves and the faithfulness of the Lord as seen in an ocean that goes so far beyond what we can see or think or imagine.

Maybe you're like me—you had to get thrown off the camel caravan and tumble down into the oasis, which was waiting for you. Your oasis may be the downtime you are now required to take due to a job loss, for example. Unstructured time to think may seem frightening at first, but it can ultimately prove to be very liberating. Just yesterday I was in my front yard, enjoying the sunset, when I saw my neighbor "Jim" walking by. Knowing he had worked for the city newspaper for years, I asked how he was doing. He stopped and said, "Well, I got laid off last month, along with two hundred other colleagues. I had worked there twenty-five years." I gasped, and then he smiled and said, "Actually, it's been wonderful. I've been writing in my journal down at the coffee shop daily, getting more clear about what I really want. As I look at what I've written, it's become clear to me that I could never have ever gotten what I *really* want by staying there."

He later showed me his journal as proof of his good thinking. "I already have three job offers, but I'm thinking over what I really want right now. I want quality of life more than anything, and this is the time for me to create that." He smiled as he walked on to his "man cave," as he calls it. He is renting a studio apartment and has his kayak permanently set on the top of his Jeep so he can take off on a moment's notice. He is intent on being restored.

Make It Yours

How do you know you need to be restored?

Here is a quick list for your review and contemplation. Check off any that apply and consider the ramifications.

- You no longer hum at work.
- You live in fear of the future.
- You are out of energy and fatigued all the time.
- You find yourself snapping at loved ones.
- You've been swimming upstream, mentally and emotionally, but not getting anywhere.
- You haven't laughed in a long time.
- Someone has broken trust with you, and now you are cautious and wary.
- People no longer come to you for ideas or opinions.
- Your life has lost its luster.
- You feel like something is missing, but you are not sure what.

God Is in the Business of Restoration

God clearly is in the business of restoration. Take a look at what Scripture tells us:

- *Lands* (Samuel 9:7): Whatever territory you think you lost in your last job upheaval doesn't matter. God wants to restore that to you, and more. And his territory, in the grand scheme of things, is vast. There is plenty to claim as your own, where you can till the ground and harvest.

- *Health* (Ecclesiastes 2:22–23): Maybe the last job you had was killing you. Maybe a forced time-out is really what you need to restore your soul. What job on earth could be worth losing your health? How might God be calling you to change your work life to safeguard it and live out the life he intended for you?
- *Position* (Genesis 41:37–40): God is actually very sensitive to the needs of ranking in society. He just wants you to know that the only society in which rank is worth caring about is his. In many stories in Scripture, the people lost one form of ranking and were later restored to an even better position. Job, Moses, Joseph, Paul, Naomi—to name a few. And our identity in Christ is always rock solid, regardless of what comes down here on earth.
- *Money* (Genesis 42:25): Jesus told parables involving concerns of small-business owners: the shepherd who lost a sheep, the widow who lost a coin, the farmer who must pay for every seed (even those that don't grow). God wants to restore to you funds that have been lost, but remember that his timing is not always like ours, and he's far more interested in the restoration of our souls.
- *Kingdom* (John 18:36): Jesus said, "My kingdom is not of this world." Neither is yours. So much damage is done in territorial conquests, even in the workplace. Sometimes we work hard to put our names on things that later shame us. For example, just this morning I read that a group of casinos named after a celebrity devel-

oper is going into bankruptcy for the third time. This developer said he was ashamed that his name was on it. Yet ten years ago he spent many hours (and millions of dollars) to make sure that happened. Make sure your career moves are not based on ego-driven conquests that may come back to bite you. God wants to restore your sense of perspective about what is truly important—the growth of *his* kingdom. When considering any career move, remember to seek first the kingdom of heaven and keep your spiritual priorities in order.

- *Goods* (Proverbs 12:27): Proverbs tells us that "the lazy man does not roast his game, but the diligent man prizes his possessions." Here the teaching is that possessions gained though diligent efforts are to be prized. Are the "toys" you want restored earned through diligent effort, or were they just handed to you too easily? For many of us, our possessions are goods attained by the simple swipe of a credit card. In the movie *Confessions of a Shopaholic*, based on the book by Sophie Kinsella, there is a line where she is contemplating a purchase and justifies it by saying, "This would define me." God is aware of the importance and true price of goods. Are we? Many people who have been through a wilderness of job loss and hardship find their taste for material goods, well, not so tasty. I doubt that you would want all the goods you've ever owned dumped back in your front yard. Most of us can't keep track of the goods we have now.

- *Comfort* (Isaiah 57:1): I have a client who regularly delights me with his take on life. Having come out of a brief marriage where my husband forbade me to work unless it was cooking in the kitchen (long story for another book), I was interested to see how this client, who was working very hard, took it that his wife had gone shopping and then was taking a nap in the afternoon. He got off the phone and turned to me with a smile and said, "I love knowing that my wife is happy and content." I wondered if God has the same feelings for his bride (us)? I think so.
- *Lost years* (Joel 2:25): This verse is particularly potent for people who feel that they are too old or that their best years are behind them or that they have lost any chance for growth. Jesus is the *redeemer*—the bringer-back, if you will, of that which was lost. Lost years is a time-based, linear illusion that becomes an excuse for living in regret. God will have none of it. The best is always yet to come.
- *Paths to dwell in* (Isaiah 58:12 KJV): "Paths to dwell in" speaks to me about principles, habits, established ways of doing things . . . not having to reinvent the wheel. When we make a life with God through Christ, seeking to abide in him and follow his precepts, we are finding "paths to dwell in." *This is the path, walk ye in it* can be such a comforting frame of mind as we navigate career choices and forks in the road. No matter how lost we might feel in the world of business, in

God's world, we always know that God can place our next footfall.

- *All things* (Matthew 17:11): Well, that about covers it, huh? "All things." Every torn picture, every broken relationship, every jagged rip of pain caused by some mistake . . . all could-have-beens, should-have-beens, might-have-beens, if-onlys . . . all of it will ultimately be made right, or restored. So often Christians forget that all of our stories—*every one*—ultimately, has a happy ending. Why not let our todays show that?

Restoration of Self Through Restoration of Others

I know a woman who found a career by simply being kind.

Anna left a stressful, high-paying job in the Northeast to head to Sedona to "find her soul." Living on money she had saved from the sale of her home, she began to take yoga classes at a local center and found that it was just the ticket she needed to reconnect with her calm center. This particular yoga center made it a practice to do good deeds to help bring about world peace, and one of the good deeds they would do was help older people.

They learned of an elderly woman who was feeling overwhelmed by clutter, so six of them decided to spend a Saturday helping her get organized. They even brought their own boxes and filing cabinets to help her clear some space. They asked for no money but simply called themselves "Twelve Hands," and that was that.

About six months later, Anna was in a car accident that caused her to begin having anxiety attacks, as well as unexpected medical bills. While she was waiting for the insurance company to settle her claims, she decided to rent out her condo to earn extra money. This money-raising strategy left her homeless, however, so one day at yoga class she asked if anyone had a place where she could stay. The elderly woman, who was now a regular attendee, said she would love to have Anna stay with her. And stay Anna did.

As the elderly woman's care needs grew, Anna asked the family if they would be willing to pay her enough to allow her to leave her part-time job selling time-shares and become the woman's caregiver. The family readily agreed, and now Anna has a career as a full-time paid caregiver for a woman she already loves and who loves her. Anna sowed a seed of kindness. The elderly woman, my mother, Irene, returned the kindness by taking her in when Anna had a need. Then, when my mother had a need, Anna returned the kindness and found a career. It was all a beautiful circle to watch, as noble intentions led to multiplied results. Anna gave before she got and was restored by doing so.

The Background Work of Restoration

Ruth 4:15 tells us that God doesn't just want to restore any life. He wants to restore *your* life, the parts that are truly you, most satisfyingly, uniquely you.

When I was restoring a home in Phoenix to the splendor of its Frank Lloyd Wright influence, I discovered to my dismay that a new, custom-made, six-foot steel beam had to be installed before we could even begin the fun and visible work. Three years later, when the project was complete and I was showing people through the house, I would pause at the twenty-foot-long, solar-lit hallway and comment, "Up above us lies the most beautiful, expensive, custom-made steel beam you will hopefully never see."

Sometimes, in order to restore us, God has to do extensive, invisible, time-consuming work. I often wonder in amazement that the New Testament Saul was sent out to the desert and was not heard from again for *years*. God must have been doing a mighty restoration work in his soul. Through the experience, he went from being Saul, proud Pharisee and persecutor of Christians, to Paul, humbled communicator and encourager of the church.

I have a good friend, an incredible therapist, who has been working to restore the confidence, health, and self-esteem of a client who was repeatedly raped as a child by her older brother, who now happens to be a "beloved priest" in her community. She refuses to expose him, fearing that it would destroy her mother, who adores her son. In my "fire" mode, I commented, "I think she would heal faster if she could see some heads roll down the aisle." But my friend gently reminded me that when doing restoration work like this, all work must be done within that person and can never be dependent on what happens to the perpetrator of the damage. Her work with this client has taken five years. Only recently have her client's many inexplicable illnesses begun to recede. Slowly, she is being rebuilt, one beam at a time. This restoration sometimes takes intense work, specialists, money, and huge investments of time. But what is your soul worth, after all?

Make It Yours

Are you in need of restoration? healing? peace? Is something broken in you, deep down, that cannot be healed on your own? Do you need to bring a third party into the mix—a therapist who can help you get to the roots of your weeds? If so, how can you find that good therapist? Someone who will help you get beyond victimization and on to healing and wholeness? Friends, a pastor, the Yellow Pages? Decide and make a call now . . . God is calling you to restoration, and this might be the first step you need to take.

Not one person whom Jesus healed is alive today. Does this mean his healing was in vain? Or was his restoration of health a physical demonstration of God's desire to see us be whole—not only now, but in life everlasting? We must remember the promise that, ultimately, all tears will be wiped away. Joy is our destiny. The portion we claim, here on earth, is up to us.

Restoration of Our "Whole Hand"

The story of healing in Luke 6:10 reminds me of that joke about a man with a withered hand who prayed, "Dear God, please make my hand like my other hand." *Kapow!* He looked down, and he had two withered hands. He sadly surmised, *Next time, I'll be more specific.*

So many of us sense there is something we lack . . . something that will keep us from winning the contest, but our sense of lack is often because we're reaching for the wrong thing. I met a woman yesterday, who is absolutely gorgeous, lamenting the fact that she went on Millionaire Match to try to find a mate but is assuming that nobody wants someone her age anymore. I counseled her to seek someone who loves her and sees her true beauty—not someone who is a millionaire. I told her that what she needs most is loving companionship. Yet she feels, on some level, that because of her age, she now has a "withered hand."

If only we could see ourselves as Jesus sees us. If only we could present ourselves in the workplace as whole and perfect and complete. If only we didn't carry with us semi-invented baggage, arguing for our limitations before we even hit the door.

Restoration of our "withered hands" might best be accomplished by addressing our atrophied, withered minds. Which "hand" of yours would you say is withered right now? Is it your left, logical, thinking-side hand? Do you react out of emotion and never think things through? Or is it your right, creative, imaginative hand, which can't seem to draw any new ideas anymore but just hangs loosely by your side because it is withered from nonuse?

Maybe you've made some mistakes in your career past. I certainly have. But I know that Christ will restore what I perceive as my withered hand and make me able to build something beautiful again with it . . . working in harmony with what I do have . . . which is *him*.

You Were Put Here to Encourage Life

I placed this chapter on restoration in the section called "Water" because that is what water does: it sustains and restores life. In the beautiful passage of Ezekiel 47 we hear about a stream that starts small and then grows . . .

> *The man brought me back to the entrance of the temple, and I saw water coming out from under the threshold of the temple toward the east (for the temple faced east). The water was coming down from under the south side of the temple, south of the altar. He then brought me out through the north gate and led me around the outside to the outer gate facing east, and the water was flowing from the south side.*
>
> *As the man went eastward with a measuring line in his hand, he measured off a thousand cubits and then led me through water that was ankle-deep. He measured off another thousand cubits and led me through water that was knee-deep. He measured off another thousand and led me through water that was up to the waist. He measured off another thousand, but now it was a river that I could not cross, because the water had risen and was deep enough to swim in—a river that no one could cross. He asked me, "Son of man, do you see this?"*
>
> *Then he led me back to the bank of the river. When I arrived there, I saw a great number of trees on each side of the river. He said to me, "This water flows toward the eastern region and goes down into the Arabah, where it enters the Sea. When it empties into the Sea, the water*

there becomes fresh. Swarms of living creatures will live wherever the river flows. There will be large numbers of fish, because this water flows there and makes the salt water fresh; so where the river flows everything will live. Fishermen will stand along the shore; from En Gedi to En Eglaim there will be places for spreading nets. The fish will be of many kinds—like the fish of the Great Sea. But the swamps and marshes will not become fresh; they will be left for salt. Fruit trees of all kinds will grow on both banks of the river. Their leaves will not wither, nor will their fruit fail. Every month they will bear, because the water from the sanctuary flows to them. Their fruit will serve for food and their leaves for healing.

—Ezekiel 47:1–12

Imagine this scripture passage as a picture of your career. It begins under the altar, as you enter a sacred place of worship. It starts flowing in a small way and then gets deeper and wider until it becomes so deep that it is a river one cannot even wade across. "Where the river flows everything will live." "The fish will be of many kinds."

You were put here to be a blessing and to be creative and to help cocreate with God. Imagine what it would feel like if you, like the water in Ezekiel 47, made everything come alive, just by touching it. Imagine what it would be like to have created a river so deep and wide that people couldn't even cross it—that it was full of a variety of "living creatures": projects, ideas, contributions. That fisherman on both sides of the river banks made a living from it. Imagine—your ideas and projects and inspirations creating a source of income for others. And your ideas were so consecrated unto the Lord that on either side of the river were trees bearing "fruit . . . for food and . . . leaves for healing." Doesn't this sound like an incredible life's work? Do you know anyone personally whose career looks like this? Anyone in history who has done this?

And all of it because the water began underneath the altar . . . it is holy and sacred and consecrated and pure. It comes from a time and place of worship. It begins at the table, where we confess our failures, offer ourselves anew, and accept forgiveness.

As you begin your career, start at the altar.

As you continue your career, stay at the altar.

And, frankly, your career on earth will someday end, but then you will meet Christ at the altar. Will you then hear those words, "Well done, good and faithful servant"? If so, your life's work will have been a success.

Jesus, Career Counselor, wants you to be restored.

CAREER EXERCISES

Are you in God's business of restoration? Evaluate your current work life and/or your future work life by going through the following questions:

1. *Restoration of Lands*
   What territory or land is my work (or future work) helping restore? Am I engaged in helping a company

expand its territory and make an impact for the betterment of all? Am I called to work in an environment that is more organic, allowing for growth and expansion in a healthy way?

2. *Restoration of Health*
   Does my work help restore the health (mental, emotional, spiritual, or physical) of others? On another level, is my work draining the health out of me and my loved ones?

3. *Restoration of Position*
   What would it mean for God to restore my "position" careerwise? Does it mean that I will get back my old desk and corner office? Does it mean that the people who fired me will come running back, realizing they made a mistake? Or is it more about my remembering my ultimate position of authority . . . that angels await my command . . . that what I lose on earth is loosed in heaven . . . that if I ask anything in the name of Jesus, it will be done for me?

4. *Restoration of Money*
   How is what I am doing contributing to the economic prosperity of others? How does my work increase and restore abundance?

5. *Restoration of Kingdom*
   How can my work help restore righteousness, justice, and mercy to others?

   What is the kingdom work God is calling me to do?

6. *Restoration of Goods*
   Does my work restore goods to people, either through proper merchandising or import/export or otherwise? What goods do I help bring to others?

7. *Restoration of Comfort*
   Can I take part in restoring comfort to others, as a health-care aide, nurse practitioner, massage therapist, interior designer, or musician? How can what I do, or want to do, help restore the comfort of others?

8. *Restoration of Lost Years*
   Might I help restore lost years to others? A good counselor can do that, as well as someone who helps with archiving or geneology. Estate planners and financial planners do this as well. Tutors. Teach-

ers. Physical therapists. Physicians. Good, listening friends.

9. *Restoration of Paths to Dwell In*
   Is my task to help restore "paths to dwell in . . ." through educating youth or building homes for veterans? By being a chaplain in the military or a clergyperson?

10. *Restoration of All Things*
    Does my work help others see that not one item in our lives has to be left unrestored . . . damaged . . . incomplete? Can I be like the woman who says her only job in life is "to be a blessing to others"? Do I have the courage to point others to the Restorer, Christ?

11. *Restoration of "Your Life"*
    Does my work give me a sense of destiny and purpose . . . a reason to get up and get there every day? Can my work be about restoring life, like working in an adoption agency or animal rescue?

What would it look like, careerwise, for you to be restored?

A PRAYER FOR YOU

"I am in need of restoration."

Dear Lord, I am "a work" in need of restoration.
My armor is chinked. My scales have fallen off.
My soul seems to limp these days rather
than soar.
Use your architectural skills to rebuild
me, within,
and your artistic skills to make my mess
a masterpiece.
I give myself to you, at the altar, Lord. Amen.

Prayers for Specific Career Concerns

"I need to take a break from what I have been doing."

Lord, you know what it is to be bone weary.
You walked many miles and healed so many.
You preached and taught and made miracle sandwiches for people, many of whom quickly forgot you, many who actively turned on you.
But what got you started? Did you get the feeling that you wanted to do something else, like I'm having now? Maybe when you were a carpenter, making one more yoke, carving one more chair.
Something must have exploded within you or you wouldn't have, couldn't have walked out that door.
Or maybe it was a slow rising, like a well filling up that told you, "There is no more room here for my soul. I must be about my Father's business."
I feel like that too. I need a break, Lord. A sabbatical perhaps. Perhaps I have not observed the Sabbath as your gift for far too long. Perhaps I have burned my midnight oil without letting it get replenished.
Help me give myself permission to have my own Jubilee . . . the time when the land itself was given a rest and old ways of doing things ceased.
Show me how to renew myself. Help me get my

tired eyes off my feet and up to the hills from whence cometh my help.
Amen and amen.

"I am unsure which way to go."

Lord, I feel like I am supposed to know this by now. After all, I have the credentials they wanted. I got the training that was required. I showed up when I didn't feel like showing up—at college, at training school, at the job.

But somehow I can't see the direction signals clearly. Or maybe I can, but they don't feel right. I just don't know what to do.

Should I take the path of least resistance and just do what everyone is telling me to do?

Should I break out from the pack altogether and make a break for what my heart has been telling me all along?

Should I just walk alongside my mentor or even find a new one?

See how many question marks I have, Lord? I can barely give you a single clear sentence with a period at the end. Help me realize that a life lived in fear of failure is not real life at all—that you are calling me to adventure and discovery and new paths, which I myself may have to blaze. Help me not be fearful of falling or making a "fatal error" by choosing the wrong school or job or place of employment. Help me remember the fascinating career path of David, who went from shepherd to king's aide to unemployed to near homeless to military man, back to king and employer. Wow, what a wild ride he had, Lord. And you loved him and shaped him every step of the way. Help me realize that walking with you can keep me from falling. You are gracious and forgiving, and life—for most of us—is long. Help me remember that the earth itself was formed "in chaos." Help me remember that clarity can walk out of a cloud, just like Moses did with your ten clear commandments. Help me face any fears that I am allowing to cause me to be mute or paralyzed. Help me discern any golden calves that are calling me to worship and devote myself to something that can never bring life.

Your word is a light unto my heart
and a lamp at my feet.

Remind me to spend more time seeking you. Remind me that sometimes decisions are delayed because of a lack of information. Remind me that confusion is sometimes a mask hiding a deep unwillingness to have a critical conversation or confrontation with myself. Never let me excuse inaction for the sake of cowardice. Help me remember that sometimes you reveal yourself

through a cloud . . . sometimes through fire.
Hover over me, dear Lord, like you did over the waters at creation. Reveal the clear boundaries and limits that I need so I may proceed with confidence into my destiny.
Amen and amen.

"People are being laid off all around me, Lord, and I'm scared."

This morning my boss called me to an early meeting and told me that he is leaving. He didn't say he was being laid off. I think the word he used was "restructuring." He had a tremble in his hand and tears welled up in his eyes as he spoke, even though he tried to be brave about it. I know he is scared. And frankly, Lord, so am I.
Will I be next? If so, where will I go? I've focused so much of my time and energy just doing the tasks in front of me and, I trust, doing them well. I haven't sought greener pastures. Should I be seeking them now? How do I get over the fear? How do I shake the pall that has seemed to settle over the office . . . the entire industry in fact. Help me remember now more than ever that you are my Rock and my Guardian. I do not lean on reeds. You created me and know my every movement, my goings in and my goings out as

the psalmist David wrote. I stand ready to serve you. I will drink now with one eye on the horizon, as all good warriors are taught to do. I will be open to new opportunities. I will sharpen my skill sets. Renew old contacts. And meanwhile serve here faithfully until I am called to serve elsewhere. Your army is huge. You will make a place for me, I know.

Help me be a source of comfort, inspiration, and strength to those around me. Let them say, "I can tell you have been with Jesus, and I want you to tell me more." Let me preach the gospel without ever needing a stage or a microphone. Let me be your words, made flesh, in every circumstance and surrounding.

Amen and amen.

Potential Relationship Skills/Water Occupations

Every personality type needs to restore, reflect, and renew, but Water personality types especially will thrive where they can nurture harmonious relationships in industries like these:

- Environment
- Fine Arts
- Parks and Recreation
- Wellness
- Acting
- Counseling

- Family Services
- Public Relations
- Social Entrepreneurs
- Travel/Hospitality/Tourism
- Writing
- Office Services
- Customer Relations
- Hospital Management
- Geriatric Care
- Commercial Art
- Health Care
- Education
- Faith and Service Organizations
- Government

Summary Points

REFLECT: Take the time to think about what is really important to you.

RENEW: What could you polish up in your life to make it shine again, like a skill set or an attitude?

RESTORE: What might you do careerwise to help restore others, just as Christ restores you.

PART III

Character Traits and Habits
Earth

Build your house upon a rock.

MATTHEW 7:24

The Earth personality type is solid, predictable, and dependable. It is organized, disciplined, and secure.

Earths take on the heavy burdens of others and work without fanfare or glory.

Earths thrive on information, data, and accuracy.

They are grounded, stable, conscientious, and prepared.

Earths tend to be efficient, factual, realistic, and modest.

Earths desire accuracy and structure in all things.

The God who created earth, wants you to remain, return, and regenerate.

CHAPTER SEVEN

REMAIN

remain 1 a: to be a part not destroyed, taken, or used up <only a few ruins *remain*> **b:** to be something yet to be shown, done, or treated <it *remains* to be seen> **2:** to stay in the same place or with the same person or group; *especially*: to stay behind **3:** to continue unchanged

This concept of "remaining" is among the most challenging for me, a Wind/Fire, to write about, because I have little natural understanding of the value of staying in one place. Recently I calculated that I have lived in seventeen different houses in ten different cities. I move around a lot, attributing it to many things, including my desire for constant stimulation mixed with solitude.

However, as I think about it now, I really owe my life and my sanity to those people who remained in one place . . . my parents who stayed in one home for thirty-seven years, allowing me a constant and steady neighborhood of friends. My friend Catherine has kept the same phone number for the thirty-plus years we have known each other. More than the same phone number, I know that no matter what is going on, or where I am, she remains there for me—available as a constant and steady voice.

Remain in Him, First and Foremost

So how does "remaining" apply to your career? What does Jesus think about the concept? Evidently, quite a lot, as in one passage in the book of John he uses the word *ten* times.

Make It Yours

Circle all the times you read the word *remain* in the scriptures below. Take a moment to absorb the content of what Jesus is saying in each instance about *remaining* by underlining other key words in each statement.

Remain in me, and I will remain in you. Just as the branch cannot bear fruit by itself, unless it remains in the vine, so neither can you unless you remain in me.

I am the vine; you are the branches. The one who remains in me—and I in him—bears much fruit, because apart from me you can accomplish nothing. If anyone does not remain in me, he is thrown out like a branch, and dries up; and such branches are gathered up and thrown into the fire, and are burned up. If you remain in me and my words remain in you, ask whatever you want, and it will be done for you. My Father is honored by this, that you bear much fruit and show that you are my disciples.

Just as the Father has loved me, I have also loved you; remain in my love. If you obey my commandments, you will remain in my love, just as I have obeyed my Father's commandments and remain in his love. I have told you these things so that my joy may be in you, and your joy may be complete.

—John 15:4–11 (NET)

As I read through this passage I was stunned at how insistent he was about the importance of *remaining*. He wasn't just saying "stay close to me, it may get tough out there." He said "*remain in me.*" The visual of the vine and the branches being one and the branch being unable to bear fruit unless it remained connected to the vine is so powerful. Think about it. If you were a branch and chose to separate from the vine, what would happen? You'd wither, shrivel, and bear no fruit at all.

Remain in One Place?

I know people who bounce in and out of relationships like popcorn.

Maybe you're one of those people.

I know people who bounce in and out of churches like jumping beans. People who bounce in and out of jobs like fleas on a dog, always trying to find a better "draw."

What would it be like to find a career or a place of work that was so fertile and comfortable and nourishing that you decided to remain there for thirty years? It can happen. And when it does, it is amazing, spiritual, scriptural. And it allows so many other things to happen as a result of it.

Listen to the blessing that can happen when we keep our hearts and minds open at all times . . . when our gates *remain* open: "Your gates will remain open at all times. They will not be shut during the day or at night, so that the wealth of nations may be delivered, with their kings leading the way" (Isaiah 60:11).

Here's what might happen if we do nothing to take delivery of the blessings God wants to bestow.

> *Angel:* I was trying to make the delivery of blessings, Lord, but the gates did not remain open . . . nobody was home. Shall I try again later?
>
> *Lord:* No . . . knowing them, they've probably moved on, still praying for joy to find them.

Note that in the Isaiah 60 passage, the gates remain open, but Isaiah does not speak of leaving the city.

I am blessed to know several incredible leaders who have remained with their companies for more than twenty-five years. In contrast to the fly-by-nights, grass-is-greener crowd, these leaders remind me of the next person we see *remaining* in Scripture: "I will stand at my watch post; I will remain stationed on the city wall. I will keep watching, so I can see what he says to me" (Habakkak 2:1 NET).

The faithfulness of the sentry is an important concept. The sentry was supposed to *remain* where he was stationed in order to keep the people safe and also to be able to receive God's word. The person who remained at his post was able to see things that were happening far away. People below inquired of him, and he was able to report what he saw. All of this was possible because he remained faithful, because he simply *remained* where he had been stationed.

My friends who have remained in their posts have grown leaders beneath them and adapted their companies to the changing times. They have built a city of refuge for employees and patients and customers and families alike. They have contributed mightily to their community in thought, word, and deed.

They have not made short-term decisions under pressure or by sniffing every trend in the wind. They have remained faithful. They have stood on guard, listening, prepared for what the Lord is telling them. "Once more a remnant of the house of Judah will take root below and bear fruit above" (2 Kings 19:30).

When it comes to your career choices, do not always assume that you have to hop around from one place to another to make a difference. If you're about to leap again, carefully study the land you are about to plant yourself in. Is it a culture that will sustain you? Nurture you? Grow you? Or is it a place that will use you up and spit you out? I have seen both kinds of places, and I'm sure you have, too. Choose wisely so you can invest in a "city" long-term.

According to a March 2009 *USA Today* poll, do you know what the number one concern of CEOs is? Talent retention. This is in the midst of massive layoffs, shrinking bank accounts, and uncertain market futures. CEOs want the talented people on their team to *remain*. Why? Because they are the ones who bear fruit.

People who bear fruit have the lifeblood of the company flowing through their veins. They can identify solutions to problems as they arise. Indeed, such people were the only asset Jesus asked to have transferred into Paradise with him. "Father, these were your gifts, and you gave them to me. And I have not lost any of them . . . and I ask that they go with me into Paradise" (Author paraphrase, John 17:6–18).

Even Jesus wanted his talented team to *remain* with him. If you are a CEO and/or manager of a team, how can you get the people to *remain*?

Each of the four personality types—Earth, Wind, Fire, and Water—has immeasurable talents to offer. A wise people manager understands the gifts of all four and how best to work with them. Right now I am consulting with a very large financial institution that has a Wind on the team who is functioning so far outside her job description that people can't find her half the time. She technically is supposed to be running the IT department but is rarely in the office. At lunch one day the CEO and CFO were talking about talent management on the team. They mentioned this lady and said, "We let her do whatever she wants. The results she gets are astounding. We don't know how she does it. But mostly we just stay out of her way." She has been at this company for fourteen years. Even Winds can remain in one place, if they are allowed freedom to move within the organization.

Remaining Gives Us Roots

When you remain in one place, you can put down roots. When you remain in one place, you can concentrate on growing in three directions at once; *down* into the soil to strengthen you against the winds that come, *up* into the sky to stretch and grow, and *around and around* as your influence and circumference expand.

I saw an amazing piece of art recently in a Santa Fe gallery. Painted on a large tree trunk slice, it shows a man in a boat, navigating the rings of change. It is said that one can judge many things by looking at the rings on a tree. "This was a rainy year.

This was a lean year." The rings of change, growing at various speeds, but always growing because the tree remained connected to its roots.

We live in a throwaway society, always quick to throw the old out in favor of the new. We travel so much perhaps because we think the next town will be prettier . . . or give us peace . . . or bring us rest.

Jesus didn't travel much beyond the nearby towns and neighborhoods. It is amazing to walk among the stone ruins of Capernaum. You see how small the villages were. There is even an inscription on a stone where the "Sons of Zebedee" had their home . . . before they got recruited by the carpenter. Jesus remained faithful in all he did. And oddly enough, he also remained in the heart of where he came from, in his homeland, working hard to make a difference in the lives of the people around him. They say he never went more than 150 miles from his home.

He bore much fruit because he remained . . . true to who he was, true to where he came from, and true to the land that birthed him and gave him so much joy.

One of my friends is a principal at an elementary school. She was named Teacher of the Year and Bilingual Teacher of the Year when she taught at this school before she went on to run it. She has been there for fifteen years, shepherding 35 teachers and 750 children. People have asked her to take her talent "higher." She says, "I am exactly where God has called me to be. I plan to remain." How blessed that community is because of her happiness to stay in one place.

I know another man, an Anglican priest, who now conducts Sunday services in a small chapel attached to a house in New

Mexico. The room holds fifteen people. Twelve were at the service I attended, including the elderly piano player who owns the home. When I asked this priest, who is handsome and articulate and very "with it," if he intended to try to grow this church, he smiled and said, "I am called to these people . . . this neighborhood. I plan to remain." Twelve people are being blessed and shepherded by this man. Just like Jesus.

What If You Can't Remain?

I know this chapter is probably tough to read if you've lost your job. But your job now is to focus on remaining in Christ and finding out where he is leading you. Or what if your job has become impossible, untenable? Here are some tips to consider:

1. Recognize that nothing lasts forever. Eventually, you would leave, anyway, even if only through death!
2. Trust God's good-making ability. Something good will surely come from this as you stay faith filled.
3. Exit gracefully, with no drama or blame.
4. Buy a kaleidoscope. Write down which pattern is the prettiest. Note that it's all the same pieces that make all those different patterns, just set in different positions.
5. Realize life is a circle of blessing. You might end up as your boss's boss someday (like Joseph). You just never know what God has planned.

Today I heard from William, a young man who has been working in a fast-paced Fortune 500 company, training its constantly changing sales team. This morning he called to say his boss let him go. When I asked him what he planned to do next, he said, "I think I want to open a grocery store here in town." No matter what has happened to him, he feels a desire to *remain in the area.*

Home Can Be a State of Mind

But sometimes we *can't* stay—even in the neighborhoods or cities we have come to love. I know how that goes—and I also know what it feels like to be called to new places, new adventures. Through it all, God has been teaching me that remaining is a state of mind—and heart. The apostle Paul, a fellow Wind/Fire, wrote, "I have learned in whatever state I am, to be content" (Philippians 4:11 NKJV). Now, Paul might have been speaking of the state of his emotional being, but I think it can apply to physical states, too. Whether I'm in California or the Carolinas—whatever state I'm in, I'm called to be content. Because wherever I am, Christ is also. I remain a branch connected to the Vine, so I am never alone, never far from home.

And so I pray for William, this young man now in a swirl of laid-off friends, and I pray for the CEO who had to make the decision to let him go. And I know in my heart of hearts that William will bear much fruit in his town . . . in his little grocery store. People always need to eat. People always need a store they can count on to remain open when hunger calls. Just like Jesus did.

Jesus, Career Counselor, wants you to *remain.*

CAREER EXERCISES

1. How long have you “remained” where you are: In your job? In your city?

2. What part does the word “faith” play in the concept of “remaining”?

3. How many people do you know who have quit too soon at a job, a career search, a relationship? What might have been the benefit if they had “remained”?

4. Do you understand what it really means to “remain in Christ”? To be a branch of his vine? If so, how can you put that more in play at your current/future job? If you don’t understand this concept, who could you go to in order to explore it further?

A PRAYER FOR YOU

"I need your peace and security."

Dear Lord, My mind and heart go
racing far from you—
in fear, distraction, or
uncertainty. Help me to
remain calm in you,
knowing that my lot
is secure in you.
Amen.

CHAPTER EIGHT

RETURN

return 1 a: to go back or come back again <*return* home> **b:** to go back in thought, practice, or condition: **revert 4:** to bring in (as profit): **yield 5 a:** to give or perform in return: **repay** <*return* a compliment>; *also*: to respond to in kind <*returned* his calls> **b:** to give back to the owner

Of all the words researched in this book regarding Scripture references, the word *return* has the highest word count. It is mentioned 568 times in the Old Testament and 125 times in the New Testament.

Word counts are a forensic tool, if you will, for researchers and authors because they denote a pattern of thinking, an emphasis of thought or concern, evidence of what is on the writer's mind. Speechwriters are sometimes given a theme to convey for their candidates. "Be sure this concept comes through" says the policy adviser. Hence the word "freedom," for example, may be used more than twelve times in a ten-minute speech. The word count denotes the message the writer wants to strongly convey.

Clearly, God wants us to hear the theme of "return" in Scripture. The concept is at the forefront of God's mind. It should also be noted that in the Old Testament it shows a people who were largely in exile, who were living and working in places that were not God's first choice for them. The overarching message seems to be "Return. Come back to me. Come back to your senses. Come back to your faith. Come back to your first love."

Return on Investment

Return is also a word of paramount importance to any employer. What will be the ROI (return on my investment) if I hire you?

What returns will you bring me? If I, like the wealthy master mentioned by Jesus, give you ten talents, will you bury them or underutilize them, leaving me less than what I began with? Or will you multiply them, giving me a worthy return? (See Matthew 25:14–30 if you're unfamiliar with the story.)

I was enlightened to a key formula when I began hiring friends and associates. It is that *each employee should generate at least three times their salary* in order to be a worthwhile investment. Why three times? Well, the first third of the money spent is for the salary itself to the employee. Then the employer pays taxes and insurance and benefits on top of that, which in some cases can be almost as much as the salary itself. That constitutes the second third. The remaining third is the profit or *return.*

Are you producing a good ROI for your employer—and your God?

Quick quiz. What does this spell? E C N A L U B M A

The puzzle would be easy to solve if you saw it in your rearview mirror. The word is AMBULANCE, and it is deliberately painted backward on the front of the vehicle because someone thought through how and where it was going to be viewed. Certainly it looked awkward to the person laying the letters out on the hood of the vehicle, but it makes perfect sense to the viewer who needs to be able to see it quickly and get out of the way.

It would be well for each person seeking a job to know how to write a résumé with backward spelling—not how it looks to them but how it is going to be viewed by the employer who needs a return. All too often we approach job opportunities from the viewpoint of what we will get from the employer, rather than considering his or her perspective—looking at us sitting there, wondering, *What will be the return for me if I hire you?*

Of course, you also need to consider *your own* return on investment for every job you take. It is wise to remember that every opportunity has a cost involved, either in lost time, lost income, or lost ability to explore other paths. For myself, I use my mission statement, vision statement, and Talent Shield as my ROI indicator.

In other words, I ask myself every time I have a new opportunity: Will this work enable me to live my mission and use my highest gifts? Is it in line with the positive vision I have for my life?

If the answer is yes to both questions, I say, "Go for it!" Anything less than 100 percent gets tabled.

Research the Return Possibilities

One way to determine what return you can bring an employer is another *R* word: *research*. This word is vital in job searches and preparing for interviews. You need to know as much about the company as possible (use Google.com or GlassDoor.com) and be aware of its financial standings (StandardandPoors.com, DunnandBradstreet.com), the industry norms (IndustryReports.com), and your salary range as compared to other job descriptions (Salaryranges.com). When you've done your research, you will be so much more prepared to serve the employer than those going in with only a vision toward their own needs and demands. Knowledge is power. With this kind of information at hand, you will be well prepared to illustrate to employers, in the short time you have, how they will make a return on their investment in you.

Your research should also include the biblical concepts of what it means to *return*. Let's look at Genesis 32:9: "Then Jacob prayed, 'O God of my father Abraham, God of my father Isaac, O Lord, you said to me, "Return to your country and your relatives, and I will make you prosper."'"

It is an interesting backstory that Jacob was a clever and gifted trickster, who was always trying to get his inheritance not by faith, but by his own might. He had thus negotiated himself into dangerous, inhospitable territory. In the verse above, God is calling him to return to his true land and calling.

Maybe this is true of you, too. Perhaps you have taken your God-given gifts and talents and used them for your own purposes—trying to get ahead, trying to wrest away something from the person you think is ahead of you, trying to outsmart and outpace God.

Let's look at Genesis 32:9 again. When you are far from home, without the people who not only support you but also hold you accountable, you are in dangerous territory. There is nothing like a cousin or brother or sister to "slap you upside your head" and say, "What were you thinking?" Those who fly beyond their means, without listening to advice, end up hitting the ground.

Many times your loving relatives are just the people you need to return to in order to get a new lease on life. Just yesterday I spoke with a friend who had gone to Vegas and then to the Northeast, putting all her investments into her own insurance agency. When the recession hit and she was forced to lay off sixty employees, she was desperate and desolate. Her sister called her from

Colorado and said, "Come home." Today, she is working at the company that has employed her sister for twenty years.

She seemingly has lost everything, yet she said she feels more at peace than she has in a long, long time. She returned to her land and to her relatives, and the Lord will prosper her there. There is absolutely nothing wrong with returning home after a career has gone "not as planned." While some of us fear returning home in defeat, the story of the prodigal son welcomed by his father gives a different biblical take on the concept.

I returned home when I was overwhelmed by a time of plenty. When *Jesus CEO* became a bestseller, I was unprepared for the sudden proposals (business and otherwise) that came flooding in. I couldn't discern between new friends who were true and those who had agendas. So I went back home where I could be with family and friends who knew me "B.CEO," as I call it.

It turned out to be just what I needed. I bought a horse ranch, as I'd promised myself I would, and spent time riding in the hills on my quarter horse rather than flying all over the place, unsure of my footing. I stayed six years and then headed back to California, when I felt called to do so.

But for a time, Jesus just wanted me to return.

Make It Yours

Are you supposed to head home? Are you being called to "come home"? Here are eight reasons to consider returning. Underline any that apply.

1. You are a stranger in a strange land—with few local connections.
2. You need the support of family and friends.
3. Your training is complete, and you want to return to help others.

4. You feel lost—with no sail up and no wind blowing.
5. Like the prodigal son (daughter), you've come to your senses after eating and sleeping with the pigs.
6. Your parents/children/grandparents/others need you.
7. Local colleges are less expensive and put less strain on the family.
8. You are really homesick.

Now let's read that verse one more time, for a still deeper look: "Then Jacob prayed, 'O God of my father Abraham, God of my father Isaac, O LORD, you said to me, "Return to your country and your relatives, and I will make you prosper."'"

The more layered look I want to take with you is this:

- *Country* represents the territory of your mission and calling.
- *Relatives* represent the gifts you have been given "relative" to or that "relate" to your mission.

I have dedicated my life to the concept and belief that each of us is created with a divine purpose. It is only as we discover that purpose and live it out in honor of God that we will find true happiness. Jesus said the same thing: "Seek his kingdom, and these things will be given to you as well" (Luke 12:31).

As I stated in the beginning of this book in "A New Vision for Your Life's Work," it is a real time and energy saver to write your mission statement and your vision statement before you begin any job search. It is also instructive to understand your highest gifts "relative" to your mission, and endeavor to remain in them at least 85 percent of the time.

How far have you strayed from your "country" or mission? How many "relative" gifts are you not using as you go about your work? If you will return to your country (mission) and the use of your gifts related to that mission, God will prosper you with peace.

Return to the Worthy

"Whatever town or village you enter, search for some worthy person there and stay at his house until you leave. As you enter the home, give it your greeting. If the home is deserving, let your peace rest on it; if it is not, let your peace return to you" (Matthew 10:11–13). The greeting Jesus mentions is one that was given in concrete fashion to an entity. If the entity proved unworthy of the peace, the blessing returned to its original conveyor.

If you were to look at this scripture in light of career choices, it also makes great sense. Whatever job or workplace you go into, seek out someone worthy and stay with her or him. In other words, go find a worthy mentor or work companion to hang around. The workplace itself deserves a blessing because you are staying there. If it does not or cannot receive the blessing because it is not worthy of you, then the blessing will return to you.

Jesus is telling us that not all places we go to will receive our blessing. In that case, we are instructed to leave, shaking off the dust from our feet (see Matthew 10:14).

Don't let the negative energy of a workplace affect you for any longer than it takes to walk out the door or city gate. Some people I know are so bitter from their last place of employment that they can't even see straight to look for another place of work. Your blessing will return to you when you leave it. In truth, if you heed these words, you have not lost anything by being there.

Returns After Loss

This is among the favorite passages on God's concept of return: "Return to your fortress, O prisoners of hope; even now I announce that I will restore twice as much to you" (Zechariah 9:12). For our discussions, I hear that as, "Return to the stronghold, O you who have felt imprisoned in the wrong workspace, mentally and spiritually, and I will return double what was taken from you."

The same return was given to Job, when he received double what he had lost as a result of his trials and tribulations. Joseph was stripped of his coat of many colors by his jealous brothers, but God returned to him abundance beyond imagining. The widow housing Elijah risked the one jar of oil she had left, and God returned to her tenfold the blessing. Even our tears will be turned into joy. We will receive a return of joy for all our sorrow. Who wouldn't want a boss who promises that? One who is always looking for ways to *return* blessing to us?

In the case of the scripture above, we can see "fortress" as faith, obedience, perseverance, and freedom from doubt. It can also mean knowing whose fortress you are in and resting in that fact. No matter how many prison-bar shadows fall across your face, they are only shadows, really, when you turn to face the Light.

Jesus, Career Counselor, wants you to *return.*

CAREER EXERCISES

1. Have you ever needed to return to God after journeying to a distant "land"? Do you need to do so now?

2. Are you afraid of returning to a career or job you once held? If so, why?

3. Do you believe that the only people who are successful are those who leave home and never come back? Do you know anyone in your hometown you would deem successful or satisfied or fulfilled? If you can't think of *anyone*, do you think that's a symptom of a false perception or lack of truth?

4. What nobility is there in the concept of returning?

5. Think of three famous novels, movies, or stories in which the hero or heroine returned home. Could you be that person?

A PRAYER FOR YOU

"I don't know if I'm supposed to return home—
literally or figuratively."

Dear Lord, I'm not sure if I'm
supposed to return home—
to the people I once knew or the job I once had.
I know you sent Moses back to Egypt
and that you are my Lord,
my God, my Commander-in-Chief.
Please send me back with wisdom and
grace and a clear purpose—
if I am supposed to go. And if you're
just calling me back to you,
help me to get past whatever blocks I have
in my life, or heart, or mind
so that I can run straight into your arms.
Let this not be a retreat or surrender,
but a return with cause. Amen.

CHAPTER NINE

REGENERATE

regenerate 1 a: to subject to spiritual regeneration **b:** to change radically and for the better **3:** to restore to original strength or properties

Danny Gregory had worked more than twenty-five years as a highly paid but unfulfilled art director. Believing in his youth the cultural myth that artists were either lazy, starving, or both, he tamped down his own artistic talents to use words to direct others.

In his book *The Creative License*, Danny shares that at the age of six he created pirate maps, "soaking them in tea for verisimilitude." He wore his Halloween costume year-round. He writes, "Twenty years later I wore ties. I only doodled when talking on the phone. I watched golf on TV." By twenty-one he said he had become rigid, unimaginative, cynical. In other words, "I was ready to get to work."

But after two decades of unfulfilling work, he opened up to some of the artists he directed (and secretly envied) about his desire to be one of them. They suggested he begin journaling again and illustrating his thoughts.

He writes, "Hesitantly, I let art back in the door. And suddenly the walls started to crack." Soon he had book contracts, requests for magazine illustrations, and a vibrant and exciting work life. He says, "I was no longer 'in management' or 'climbing the ladder.' Instead, I was me."

Danny, while living what I call a parallel career (being close to but not doing what you want to be doing), found regeneration of his first love. And he began to thrive.

In Revelation 2:4, God speaks to one of the churches and says, "Yet I hold this against you: You have forsaken your first love."

The implication, of course, is that they have forgotten Jesus. For us, careerwise, the implication might be that we have forgotten what we first loved to do, what we were gifted and endowed and actually created to become.

God is not pleased when we try to be or do something that we are not. Would you be pleased if you saw the beauty and unique talents within your children, and you set them on a track to utilize those God-given gifts in their work, but they did the opposite? I don't think so.

I believe God is calling us to regenerate our careers by returning to our first love.

Regeneration Through New Roles

Joseph Campbell, a noted author and cultural historian, said he observed that most of us identify ourselves consciously or subconsciously with a character or story and begin to live that out.

We may become the Wanderer, always seeking, never settling down.

We may become the Exiled one, trying to find a way home.

We may become the Warrior, the Slave/Victim, the Princess, or the King. Much of the path work we have done with young people in first-offender programs has to do with helping them to see that they are living out *negative* predictions and stories they have been told about themselves—with great accuracy and effort. If they can just begin to believe new stories about themselves, their actions and destinies will change.

Regeneration involves letting go of old identities, letting go of old pictures, letting go of the way things have always been/used to be, and embracing new forms. *One of the hardest things about career change is letting go of the stories we have about ourselves.*

"Destroy this temple, and I will raise it again in three days" (John 2:19). Here Jesus was speaking to people who thought they had power over him. He knew he could regenerate what others thought they could destroy. The same is true of you, in Christ.

No matter where you are, or even how old you are, there will come a time when you will need to bring forth something new out of the old . . . when what worked before doesn't seem to be enough . . . when some new razzle-dazzle is required of you.

Do you have it in you? Where will you find it?

In your Source, of course!

When we become united with the Messiah, we become one with All That Is, All That Creates, All That Knows. When we tap back into that Source, we begin to see amazing things happen in our lives. We begin to regenerate.

Recently there have been a rash of suicides among Wall Street titans who suddenly saw their scripts change and couldn't handle it. *"If I can't play the king, I don't want to play anymore,"* they seem to have said—and then they put a bullet through their brains. They did not believe they had the ability to regenerate a new and powerful story about themselves.

Naomi, in the Bible, offers a vivid example of someone whose career path was brought to a fork in the road. Suddenly bereft of her sons and husband through death, she faced an uncertain future. Unaware of how God is in the business of regeneration, she could see only a cursed existence stretching out before her, a widow forevermore alone and forgotten. But God had regeneration in store for her, and it came in the form of her daughter-in-law Ruth, who spoke these oft-repeated words in marriage ceremonies: "Whither thou goest, I will go; . . . thy people shall be my people, and thy God my God" (Ruth 1:16 KJV). God had a plan to make Naomi new again. He was able to regenerate her future. He can do the same for you.

Laid off? God's still on the job.

Retired? God is never idle.

Fired? God stands by.

Forgotten? God remembers.

Passed up? God sees.

C. S. Lewis once said, "You have never met a mere mortal." This means your capacity to accept and expand into new roles and "stories" is infinite. Open yourself up to the possibilities, and be amazed. Unite again with the Messiah, and listen to his words for you, his plans for you, his hope for you; then watch your soul (and vocation) regenerate.

Regeneration Through New Generations

Another way to regenerate your career is through multiplication of progeny—either by reproduction and fruitfulness of the breeding variety or through training and teaching of the mentoring variety. "But you have said, 'I will surely make you prosper and will make your descendants like the sand of the sea, which cannot be counted'" (Genesis 32:12).

It is a fact of life that we are all destined to die. But only our flesh will fade away. We will leave behind memories and sayings and recipes and photographs and writings and philosophies. Are you living in awareness of this? Or are you pretending that death will never knock on your door?

When I was in my high-buying real estate phase, I must have somehow imagined that the sheer number of properties I owned would grant me peace. In contrast, each apartment unit represented a toilet that would flood, a sink that would overflow, an air conditioner that would break. The more property I owned, the less I was able to sleep. One day, I accepted this fact: no matter how many thousands of square feet of buildings I owned, when I died I was ultimately going to need only six feet of soil.

It was then that I decided to regenerate myself—not through real estate but through writing, my first love. Not through trying to get great deals on property, but in helping other people discover the tremendous properties they have within themselves. And through this regenerative thinking, my peace and, interestingly enough, my economics were also restored.

From the Ashes . . . Life

God is in the business of regenerating something new from something old.

Stephanie Roy, an assistant professor at the University of Montreal, responds to the Ask.com question: How do animals regenerate? Excerpts of her response are as follows:

> Many kinds of animals can regenerate or regrow new parts of their bodies. If you cut a planarian, flat worm, or a sponge into pieces, each piece becomes an entire new entity. Starfish and lizards can lose an arm and a tail, respectively, and regrow a replacement. Sharks can lose and regrow up to 24,000 teeth over their lifespan. Crickets can regenerate their legs. These are just a few examples of invertebrates capable of regenerating complex structures. . . . Amphibians, however, have the outstanding ability to regenerate perfectly complex tissues over and over again, and each time, the regenerated tissue is identical to the original in appearance and function. The exact mechanism of how these animals can regenerate is not currently well understood.

Maybe you've just survived being fired but feel like the flat worm, cut into fifty pieces. Or perhaps you wish someone *would* fire you, sever your dead job limb. Can the God who created these creatures help regenerate you? Of course! For with God, nothing is impossible.

He's already regenerating you *physically* in ways you may not even be aware of. According to Dr. Mark Liponis, "Essentially we are all 'cancer survivors.' Mutation in the DNA of any of our 100 trillion cells occurs constantly in all of us, and new cancer cells are a common occurrence even in young adults. However these microscopic cancers almost never become lethal tumors—mostly because our immune system detects them early and snuffs them out before they have a chance to grow. Only cancer cells that develop a cloaking mechanism to evade the immune system or tumors that develop their own blood supply can successfully grow into potential lethal tumors."[3] In other words, the body and its immune system is continually regenerating healthy cells in order to assure a healthy organism.

Skin cells regenerate every twenty-one days. Hair cells regenerate. Fingernail cells regenerate. Healing is itself an act of regeneration. Is the God who created our bodies to do all of that *unable* to regenerate our careers? I think not.

Here is one of my favorite little scriptures, which contains huge kernels of truth: "A bruised reed he will not break, and a smoldering wick he will not snuff out. In faithfulness he will bring forth justice" (Isaiah 42:3).

God will not break you when you feel crushed.

He will not extinguish your tiniest remaining flame. (Others may call you a "dim wick," but God has something much greater in store for you.) When you are challenged by age or job loss or financial setbacks . . . when it seems like you have only one tiny spark left in you, offer that spark up to God. He will place his hands around it and make sure it does not go out. He will help you regenerate your flame of hope and passion and purpose. He has great plans for you indeed and will execute those plans faithfully.

How Does Your Life Taste?

Jesus said, "You are the salt of the earth. But if the salt loses its saltiness, how can it be made salty again?" (Matthew 5:13). In Roman times, workers were paid with the most valuable commodity at the time, which was salt. The word *salary* comes from this ancient form of worker payment.

Perhaps now is the time for you to think back about what it was that you were hired to do. What was it that your employer saw in you, in the early days, that turned an interview into a pay stub? While contemplating this book, it occurred to me that God really only *fired* a few people: King Saul. Selfish shepherds. Scribes and Pharisees. Stiff-necked people. Those are the ones who got the heavenly boot. And why? They refused to regenerate themselves into God-pleasing people. They refused to become new again in their hearts.

They became neither hot nor cold, but lukewarm, and got spit out (see Revelation 3:16).

They lost their passion and became useless.

These were people in ripe form for regeneration. After all, Saul became Paul, right? We're all in need of a new chapter, now and again. But it is our choice whether we allow God to transform us and make us more than we once were.

"Matter can never be destroyed. It can only be transformed." This is a law of physics. It is observable in nature, as a bud turns to a leaf then turns to mulch, which then replenishes the earth. A piece of wood that burns turns into carbon and oxygen—earth and air—which then merges with clouds and becomes rain, which waters the earth. Some might say we are in a cycle of death, with all things deteriorating toward formlessness. Yet such cynics only see half of the picture, for all things ultimately come back together. Remember, "Matter can never be destroyed. It can only be transformed"—and that includes *you*.

Regeneration as a Process

And what of us? How do we begin to regenerate?

A recent quote from Gore Vidal speaks to me of this process—how it begins. "The creation of a work of art, like an act of love, is our one small 'yes' in the center of a vast 'no.'"

Look around and you'll see evidence of how God works to regenerate, if we allow him to do so. Cut a tree down to a stump, keep it watered, give it some sun, and in a season or two you will see baby branches sprouting out of it!

Margaret Wheatley created a stir in the business world with her book *Leadership and the New Science: Discovering Order in a Chaotic World.* In it she says that systems left to themselves do not deteriorate toward chaos but ultimately toward harmony. It all depends on one's perspective. "We know that in all things God works for the good of those who love him, who have been called according to his purpose," Romans 8:28 tells us.

Regeneration for an Older Generation

Think you're simply too old for regeneration? Consider, then, Psalm 92:14: "They will still bear fruit in old age."

Think about this. Most football games are won or lost in the last two minutes of the game. There is nothing like a deadline to focus our best efforts and highest selves. Consider the thief on the cross. With his last breath he recognized Jesus and ended up with a ticket to paradise.

My friend Bob Buford has dedicated much of his life to the concept of going from "Success to Significance" and thinking about your life at "Half Time." He formed a foundation dedicated to helping people look for ways to be significant in their communities and churches, especially through the last half of life.

We may see ourselves moving toward the end of the line. But that is pre-Columbus thinking—medieval thinking—assuming that the world is flat and that we will have a final "splat" landing when we reach the end of it.

Have you ever watched the sun go down?

If you said yes, that is a WRONG ANSWER! The truth is, no, you never have seen the "sun go down," and neither have I. Because the sun isn't really moving in relation to planet Earth—we are, as we walk around on a planet that is spinning more than one thousand miles an hour. Everything is a circle. Once you and I get that concept, we will be less afraid of falling off a cliff or heading downhill.

Dick Stenbakken is a retired military colonel who has had, by my count, three full careers. He was a military chaplain in his first career. He then became head of global operations for a large church denomination, his second career. Upon recently retiring from that, he is now a media actor and producer of his self-authored series on Bible characters. In a most recent e-mail to me he wrote:

> *Last week, Monday–Wednesday, I shot seventeen thirty-minute TV shows—all interviews with various Bible characters. . . . Earlier in the month, I shot an eight-part DVD on the armor of God out of Ephesians 6, with a panel of four other very articulate guys. We did all eight segments in one day! It was a marathon, but it got done.*

Clearly, here is a man who lives the principle of regeneration. It is easy to regenerate when you are plugged into the Source of your passion. Jesus said that if we believe in him, rivers of living water will flow out of our hearts. The old King James version says they'll flow out of our "belly."

Now that is a promise God intends to keep.

Regeneration Through Crisis

In every crisis there is always the seed of equal or greater benefit.

Oral Roberts Sr. used to preach this every week on television, and my grandmother would get out her TV tray and her checkbook and eagerly listen to his words. Read those words again: *In every crisis, there is always the seed of equal or greater benefit.* The true regenerators know where to find that seed and how to nurture it.

If you're in a crisis, you need to identify the good that can come out of it. If you can't see it, get optimistic, affirming friends to help point it out. And be sure to keep a sense of perspective. When the US Airways flight recently had to do a splash landing in the Hudson River, the shaken passengers filed out onto the wing to be met by a ferry operator who said simply, "Welcome to New York." His sense of humor helped lift the mood and erase some of the fears of people who had only moments before faced near-certain death.

Crisis does not mean you'll always feel afraid, unstable, adrift. One of the things I discovered about myself is, I feared that somehow I wouldn't be safe. But underneath that fear was this one: I did not trust God to be able to keep me safe. So I was trying to build a fortress for retirement . . . but I've realized, after fifty-plus years of ups and downs and ins and outs, that—

guess what? My God is able to keep me safe because at my true core I am a spirit that is eternal, indestructible, perpetual. All the rest is drama and illusion, entertainment, training exercises, and coachable moments preparing me for eternity. That is a perspective that leads one to be able to regenerate more easily.

Some of the best growth comes through crisis. We are never more near to God than when we are on our knees, for the need to seek answers and truth beyond our own means is truly the opening Christ needs. It is the humble and broken in spirit who inherit the blessing—not the wise and all-knowing. So embrace hard times for the gifts they can be!

Make It Yours

How do you regenerate your career? Here are quick tips to help you in your regeneration process. Underline anything you think might help you get started.

- Cut it up. (Take smaller tasks/cut your hours.)
- Change it up. (Ask to be transferred to a different department.)
- Ask for more. (Take on more responsibility, management opportunities, or new projects.)
- Make it fun again. (View it as a hobby. What about this was once fun for you? How can you get back to doing that again?)
- Get a mentor. (Having someone to help talk over things can give you a new perspective.)
- Learn something new. (Learning = Growth)
- Take on a special project. (The stimulations of something out of the ordinary will fire new neurons.)
- Ask others what you are good at. (Maybe you're in a rut and can't see your new path that is obvious to others.)

(continued)

- Offer to help mentor someone else. (Their challenges and fresh approach might inspire you!)
- Other ideas:

Maybe you have been kicked in the gut by a circumstance you didn't expect. Once you catch your breath, remember that God has placed within you everything you need to regenerate your soul, and your career.

Jesus took a little boy's lunch, broke it, gave thanks, and prayed; and it was regenerated into enough food for more than five thousand people. Notice that he worked with what he had, as insignificant as it seemed. He *broke it*, meaning he changed its form. He *gave thanks in faith*, knowing that his Father had the regenerative power to make it new again, and he *prayed*, acknowledging the already existing connection. Then he sat back and watched the miracle unfold.

He can do the same for you, in your career life, right now.

> *The Lord your God is with you, he is mighty to save. He will take great delight in you, he will quiet you with his love, he will rejoice over you with singing.*
>
> —Zephaniah 3:17

Jesus, Career Counselor, wants you to *regenerate*.

CAREER EXERCISES

1. Imagine for a moment that there is a force in you that is whispering, "Live. Grow. Live. Grow." Twenty-four hours a day, seven days a week. Would this be in line with what you are hearing right now? If not, what words are echoing in the background of your life and career?

2. Think of a shattered mirror. If you glued all the pieces back together, you'd still see yourself there in its reflection, right? No matter what you've gone through, no matter how shattered you *feel*, know that you are *whole* in Christ.
3. If you understand and believe that God is the author and finisher of your faith, will you be willing to let him write a new script for you? What do you think the beginning of that script says? Write it here:

4. If you need regeneration in your current position, who could you seek out to help you brainstorm on how to do that? Name them here, and then contact them.

....

....

....

....

A PRAYER FOR YOU

"I want God to regenerate my life, passion, and work."

Father, I'm in need of regeneration on several levels. Begin with my life, Jesus. Make me new, from the inside out. Help me grab hold of your promises and live them out in faith. Fuel your call in my heart to serve you in my work. Take part in every hour of every day of my life, and make it all something uniquely yours. Amen.

CHARACTER TRAITS AND HABITS/EARTH BONUS FEATURES

Prayers for Specific Career Concerns

"I may have to relocate."

Lord, my supervisor and team are asking me to relocate. Help me discern if doing so will allow me to live my mission and stay focused on my highest gifts and priorities. Help me also to realize that relocation often brings many blessings, like new experiences, new growth, new friends and colleagues. Help me remember that many of your favorite people in Scripture were asked to relocate, also . . . like Abraham and Nohomiah, Ruth and Naomi.

Help me remember that you said, "I will be with you always." That there is no place I can go outside of you, beyond you, or too far from you. Help me remember that your Spirit is mobile, flexible, and always available, no matter where I am today, no matter where I will be tomorrow. I ask your blessing and compassion on family and friends who may experience upset or loss as a result of this call. Help me be compassionate and understanding as they process any losses, real or perceived, that they might experience because of this. Moving forward in faith and

patience, I am eager to meet you on any field, in any place, at any time. It is you I serve, you I desire, you who lives in me and through me. May I be a worthy servant.
Amen and amen.

"I am in a family business."

Dear Lord, you know the challenges that come from laboring among people who don't always see eye to eye. You yourself left a family business as a carpenter and began to work among the self-employed. My challenges here are many. I feel sometimes I am invisible, especially to my elders. They still see me as a child, I think, unable to act on my own. I feel sometimes I cannot express my gifts fully in their presence, for fear I overshadow them or make them uncomfortable.
Likewise, I am torn because sometimes I want to work elsewhere. I want to strike out on my own, free of the many obligations and encumbrances made by generations before me. I long for the open sea and a clean slate and new horizon, where nobody knows my name and I am seen for only me. If indeed you are calling me to step out from the family business, please help me be very clear about this and the mission that is mine to follow.
Lord, if I stay, help me be patient with my

siblings and in-laws who labor with me. I feel sometimes like I have to walk on eggshells not to hurt anybody's feelings. I want to fully express the gifts and ideas you have placed within me. Show me how to do this. Send us a counselor who can help us turn land mines into flower fields, free of resentments or hidden agendas. Family businesses offer so much to so many. Help me honor not only my family's name, but most especially yours in all I do and say. Amen and amen.

"I am self-employed."

Lord, not only do I have to labor now, but I also have to figure out what work needs to be done. Sometimes it seemed so much easier to have someone else's schedule or agenda to follow. At least I could leave the office and turn off the lights (and my mind) and fully declare, "It's free time now. I am off duty!"

Being self-employed means I am never really off duty now. I am multitasking in so many ways, many times in areas that are unfamiliar and uncomfortable for me. I truly cannot show up anywhere and just coast through the day, knowing my paycheck is secure. I must always be alert for any danger or opportunities on the horizon. I feel like I have a cell phone in one hand and a sword in the other.

Where is room for the cross?

When I look at nature, I see how wonderfully "self-employed" the lilies of the field are. They seem to blossom without effort, trusting themselves to the seasons of you. The birds of the air have no bosses to speak of, and yet you know when even one of them falls. Help me to remember this as sometimes I isolate myself and think nobody can understand the troubles that I see.

Help me remember to congregate with others of like feather at the end of the day, just as I see the sparrows on a wire, gathering at sunset. Sometimes they don't seem to engage with one another but just position themselves on the wire and behold the magnificence of the end of the day. Maybe they are praying, too, in their own way, thanking you for making sure that they got fed another day and were able to put their wings to use. Help me remember that self-employed birds sing while they work. Self-employed bees hum while they work, too.

Help me experience the deep contentment that knows you are the heaven I seek, the heart I serve, and the longing that I respond to as I deliver my gifts to the world.

I adore you as I rest my wings, and also as they rise.

Amen and amen.

"I am too old to start over."

Dear Lord, okay. I know I am talking to someone ageless here. I realize that some of your best work was done with people in their eighties. I realize that "retirement" was never a promise you made, but one which I bought into—even sought before its time. Help me to regenerate myself, like some of the simplest beings in nature. Help me to be relevant since I can speak from wisdom and experience and have stayed current with the times. Ignite a new passion in me to get even more current. Help me not isolate or withdraw, thinking others will not respect me. Help me see each wrinkle as a "magnificent scent-gathering device" that is praised in bloodhounds and other hound dogs that hunt.

Oh Lord, I once heard that a wise person never cuts down a tree in winter, for new life may always spring again. Put a new spring within me. Help me find new ways to serve. In your kingdom nothing is wasted and is never really destroyed. Help me see myself as valued by you and valuable to others. Help me make laughter my best medicine and faith in you the smile I wear. Amen and amen.

Potential Character Traits and Habits/Earth Occupations

Every personality type needs to remain, return, and regenerate, but Earth personality types especially will thrive where they can deliver data, structure, and accuracy in industries such as these:

- Architecture
- Corrections
- Environment
- Restaurant Management
- Sports Management
- Entrepreneur (might need to pair with Fire or Wind for promotion)
- Consultant
- Politics
- Athletics
- Project Engineers
- Finance
- Real Estate
- Systems Design
- Urban Planning
- Manufacturing
- Energy
- Health Care
- Education
- Faith and Service Organizations
- Mass Media
- Government
- Nonprofits

Summary Points

REMAIN: Sometimes the grass really isn't greener on the other side. Perhaps God wants you to stay in one place in order to receive the blessing.

RETURN: There is no shame in turning around and going back to what you knew, what you once loved, where you once lived. Perhaps God is calling you home in new and exciting ways.

REGENERATE: Even an old stump will spring forth with new shoots. It is within us to keep regenerating life, including new ideas out of old ones.

PART IV

Creativity and Innovation

Wind

Awake, north wind,
and come, south wind!
Blow on my garden,
that its fragrance may spread abroad.

SONG OF SOLOMON 4:16

Wind personality types have an active, curious intellect. They are the messengers, bringing hints of spring as well as the scent of fire.

Winds are playful, out-of-the-box thinkers who see new ideas everywhere.

Winds easily transcend all boundaries.

They are optimistic, charming, amusing, and spontaneous.

The God who created the wind wants you to revive, release, and rejoice.

CHAPTER TEN

REVIVE

revive 1: to restore to consciousness or life **2:** to restore from a depressed, inactive, or unused state: **bring back 3:** to renew in the mind or memory

When I was about ten years old, I discovered a hummingbird lying outside our picture window. It's little tongue was hanging out, and its eyes were closed. I gently took it in the palm of my hand and held it while I cried. I didn't want the ants or a cat to get it, so I just held it, like children do. When I finally stood up to go tell my mother we needed to bury the bird, it suddenly perked its little head up, shook once or twice, and then flew away.

My eyes were as wide as the saucers on the kitchen counter when I went in stammering, "Mom, I think I just brought a bird back to life!" Looking down at my hands, I began contemplating how the power to raise the dead might affect my writing career, which I had earlier declared. I felt her put her arms around me and say, "Honey, that was a wonderful thing to behold. You did a good thing lifting it off of the ground. But the bird was just stunned, not dead. By holding it in your hand, you gave it time to be revived." With that she kissed my head and walked away. I sat down slowly at the counter, brushing my hands on my blue jeans, relieved that I could become a writer after all.

Maybe you are like a bird that has flown into a glass wall. It looked clear ahead. All the signs were there that you could continue on your flight path, and you were going at it full speed, when *whack!* The next thing you know you are on the ground, tongue hanging out, eyelids half closed.

You might feel stunned into silence, submission, inaction, defeat. You need to be revived.

Just Breathe

Revival begins with catching your breath again. You have taken a fall. The fact is, we all move too fast these days. And we don't wear the right protective devices at all. In the aftermath of the tragic death of movie star Natasha Richardson, people across the world were stunned that a woman in the prime of her life could fall while skiing on a baby slope, hit her head, and die as a result of an undetected brain hemorrhage. A neurologist who was summoned to one media station explained, "The human skull was designed so that it can protect the fragile brain at speeds up to fifteen miles per hour, which is about how fast an average human can run for any period of time. The skull was not designed to protect the brain from falls at speeds in excess of that. Which is why slowing down, and/or helmets are required."

I can just see God designing the first human beings, saying to the angels, "Surely they wouldn't go faster than that. After all, we've reserved the wings for the birds." However, in our culture and society, we do go faster than we were designed to go—all the time, and in multiple ways.

The story is told about a group of Americans who made a trip down the Amazon River with some Brazilian natives. After three days of rushing to their destination, on the fourth day, the Americans were surprised when the natives sat together in a circle. When asked why the natives weren't moving, the guide answered, "They are waiting for their souls to catch up with their bodies."

Consider the History of Revival

The word *revival* figures prominently in American history. The tent would go up, the preacher would come to town, the music would swell, and soon the people would start to shout and stomp and cry. They would pray and then en masse throng forward toward the stage, giving their lives to God (and their money to the preacher).

Have you ever been to a revival? It is an exciting thing to see. One of my favorite memories was a revival I attended in the Caribbean. I was actually invited to preach there. I finally spoke about three hours after I was scheduled to speak, largely because in the islands there is a British-informed formality that is enhanced by the freedom people feel to speak their minds.

The armor bearer introduces the aide in arms who then introduces the honorable committee chairperson who then introduces the beloved speaker, after acknowledging every person in that reverse chain and their families. Every person on the stage feels the call to be a preacher. Scripts are frowned upon as that would inhibit the Holy Spirit.

So, I vaguely remember taking the podium in the wee hours of the morning when I had been scheduled for the dinner keynote. Not that I minded. It was an amazing experience to be in that revival setting.

As I recall, sometime near or during my keynote, one lady began to prophesy. She called out a man from the audience to come forward and then proceeded to prophesy that the Holy Spirit wanted to rid him of the demon of laziness. She then drew her little white-lace-gloved hand back and punched him hard in the stomach. He doubled over, and as her hand opened up to slap that demon out of him, he deftly (and wisely) fell back, dodging a blow that would have surely "revived" him. I was amused to learn later that this lady prophetess was also this man's boss, so she must have had some added insight from the Lord about his work habits. I do believe he arose from that floor "revived."

With all affectionate humor aside, sometimes it takes an event to revive us. Sometimes we need to buckle at the knees before the pastor can bring the smelling salts. "Wake up!" Jesus urges us. "Get a new life in you!"

My personal revivals have not come in large crowds, but rather in quiet moments when, for some inexplicable reason, a hush falls over me. I know that God is in the room—his holy presence is near. It used to happen in moments of awe, but now rather frequently happens when something tickles me. I especially seem to get revived around dogs and children. Their innocence, their profound grasp of when I need a hug or a kiss on the nose, for example, helps me remember that God's love comes in many forms and that his presence is always near.

Gideon had his own revival through a very personal encounter with a stranger. Note how casually the angel observed and interacted with Gideon where he was.

> *The angel of the Lord came and sat down under the oak in Ophrah that belonged to Joash the Abiezrite, where his son Gideon was threshing wheat in a winepress to keep it from the Midianites. When the angel of the Lord appeared to Gideon, he said, "The Lord is with you, mighty warrior."*

(Note that God sees us, even when we are trying to hide from him!)

> *"But sir," Gideon replied, "if the LORD is with us, why has all this happened to us? Where are all his wonders that our fathers told us about when they said, 'Did not the LORD bring us up out of Egypt?' But now the LORD has abandoned us and put us into the hand of Midian."*
>
> *The LORD turned to him and said, "Go in the strength you have and save Israel out of Midian's hand. Am I not sending you?"*
>
> —Judges 6:11–14

God ignores Gideon's excuse and says, "Go in the strength you have." Gideon had a revival in the form of a personal message from God. *"No excuses now, just go!"* Gideon, even while hiding from responsibility and conflict, could not escape the loving and empowering gaze of God. I love the line, "Go in the strength you [DO] have." God will take our feeble breaths and turn them into roars.

Even When All Seems Lost . . . Believe

Joseph, a young man full of dreams and promise and his father's favor, still ran across times of need for revival. Notice how many discouraging and "bad" things happened to him on his career path. Notice also how many times there was a new wind blowing into his life that carried him to the next level. He got revived over and over (and over) again.

Now Israel loved Joseph more than any of his other sons, because he had been born to him in his old age; and he made a richly ornamented robe for him. . . .

Joseph had a dream, and when he told it to his brothers, they hated him all the more. . . .

So when Joseph came to his brothers, they stripped him of his robe—the richly ornamented robe he was wearing—and they took him and threw him into the cistern.

—Genesis 37:3–5, 23–24

This looked like the first end of Joseph's dream of a career path. However, there was no water in the cistern, and a kinder brother, Judah, rescued him and convinced his brothers to sell him as a slave instead of leaving him to die. "So when the Midianite merchants came by, his brothers pulled Joseph up out of the cistern and sold him for twenty shekels of silver to the Ishmaelites, who took him to Egypt" (Genesis 37:28).

Joseph prospered in Egypt and looked like he had a terrific career ahead of him, until another setback occurred—this one in the form of a deceitful woman. She declared falsely that Joseph had tried to rape her. "When his master heard the story his wife told him, saying, 'This is how your slave treated me,' he burned with anger. Joseph's master took him and put him in prison . . . [but] the LORD was with Joseph and gave him success in whatever he did" (Genesis 39:19–23). This included the ability to interpret dreams! After a while, powerful men began to seek his counsel.

When two full years had passed, Pharaoh had a dream he didn't understand.

Then Pharaoh said to Joseph, "Since God has made [my dreams] known to you, there is no one so discerning and wise as you. You shall be in charge of my palace, and all my people are to submit to your orders. Only with respect to the throne will I be greater than you. . . ."

Then Pharaoh took his signet ring from his finger and put it on Joseph's finger. He dressed him in robes of fine linen and put a gold chain around his neck. He had him ride in a chariot as his second-in-command, and men shouted before him, "Make way!" Thus he put him in charge of the whole land of Egypt.

—Genesis 41:39–40, 42–43

Notice how many times in the story that it seemed like Joseph was finished. Dead on arrival. His bright dreams had gotten him nowhere. Yet God revived him every time, even as Joseph continued to do his work each day, no matter where he was or the negative circumstances surrounding him. God intends to faithfully reach out to you, find you, and revive you no matter where you are.

Dry Bones Brought to Life

I want to close this chapter with one of the most beautiful passages of revival in Scripture. It is from Ezekiel chapter 37, and it answers the question, "Can these bones live?"

The hand of Yahweh was on me; he carried me away by the spirit of Yahweh and set me down in the middle of the valley, a valley full of bones. He made me walk up and down and all around among them. There were vast quantities of these bones on the floor of the valley; and they were completely dry. He said to me, "Son of man, can these bones live?" I said, "You know, Lord *Yahweh." He said, "Prophesy over these bones. Say, 'Dry bones, hear the word of Yahweh. The* Lord *says this to these bones: I am now going to make breath enter you, and you will live. I shall put sinews on you, I shall make flesh grow on you, I shall cover you with skin and give you breath, and you will live; and you will know that I am Yahweh.'" I prophesied as I had been ordered. While I was prophesying, there was a noise, a clattering sound; it was the bones coming together. And as I looked, they were covered with sinews; flesh was growing on them and skin was covering them, yet there was no breath in them. "He said to me, Prophesy to the breath; prophesy, son of man. Say to the breath, 'The* Lord *Yahweh says this: Come from the four winds, breath; breathe on these dead, so that they may come to life!'" I prophesied as he had ordered me, and the breath entered them; they came to life and stood up on their feet, a great, an immense army.*

Ezekiel 37:1–10 (NJB)

This passage was written by a prophet of God who was given a vision of revival. You, too, may be in need of such a vision. Perhaps the valley of your life is full of old, dry bones . . .

Dry bones of a career that used to be vibrant and alive but is now stale and boring.

Dry bones of a dream to make a difference in the world, but somehow that dream never got enough muscle around it to do anything.

Dry bones of an image you once had of yourself as a person of might and power and substance.

Dry bones of a business idea that never quite got off the ground.

No matter your scenario, these words, from another of God's prophets, are true for you:

Those who hope in the Lord
will renew their strength.
They will soar on wings like eagles;
they will run and not grow weary,
they will walk and not be faint.

—Isaiah 40:31

The very breath of God is in your soul and is far greater than the world, which currently may seem to overwhelm you. The breath of God is yours to inhale. The kiss of the Lord is on your lips.

Jesus says to you now, "Arise!"

Jesus, Career Counselor, wants you to be *revived.*

CAREER EXERCISES

1. Describe what in your life needs revival right now: Write it here:

2. Have you been sucker punched in the gut and can't catch your breath, feeling only raw pain and shock? Have you become a valley full of old, dry bones, not even connected like they once were? Think about what happened *after* the last time you felt this way (or anywhere close to it). Can you find hope in the story you've already lived?

3. How about getting up and going out early to seek him, instead of staying where you are, paralyzed, afraid, exhausted? What could you do to get closer to God for an hour each morning—even if it's just for this special time of seeking revival? Describe your plan here:

A PRAYER FOR YOU

"I'm too dry and dusty to summon
the strength for revival."

Dear Lord, my energy is spent. I want to do the right thing and follow you wherever you lead me. Revive my soul. Breathe your sweet breath upon me. Make these dry bones rise up like a great army. Amen.

CHAPTER ELEVEN

RELEASE

release 1: to set free from restraint, confinement, or servitude **4:** to give permission for publication, performance, exhibition, or sale of; *also:* to make available to the public **synonyms:** see *free*

Many have pondered why Jesus asked the rich young man to go and sell, or release, everything he owned and give it to the poor, yet did not require that specifically from any of his other followers. I think one reason was that the young man was so bound up in what he owned that he couldn't experience the freedom that comes from having nothing left to lose.

Release. It is such a beautiful, profound word.

As I'm sitting here working on this chapter at a local restaurant, the ever-present sports channel is on multiple television sets. It occurs to me that every sports hero knows how to release.

Pitchers have to release the ball to be great.

Hitters have to release their swing to connect.

Basketball players run down the court for the sole purpose of releasing the ball into the hoop.

Quarterbacks have to release the ball every time it is given to them or, frankly, they get hurt.

Every sports hero I can think of is a master at the art of release.

Are you releasing your gifts in your work? Or do you choke, afraid to swing? Do you hoard the ball, thinking you might never get another chance to throw? Do you keep dribbling on the court, never releasing that ball toward the hoop? If so, how long do you think any team will want you?

Jesus had strong and angry words for the servant who buried his talents. Are you faithfully releasing your tithes and offerings and gifts? If not, you are holding up blessings in heaven. God cannot use miserly hearts. Jesus actually cursed a fig tree that refused to bear fruit.

To the one who releases much, more will be given.

Those who hoard and hang on to the gifts they have received don't go anywhere.

Know When to Release

One of the most important concepts to understand about release is knowing *when* to let go. If you have ever tried to take something from a two-year-old, you know that we humans tend not to release something in our hands until we are offered something else we perceive to be better.

Songs like "Stuck on You" convey a visual that is not attractive, and yet we tend to think that the objects of our affection offer us life itself. This could be true about job descriptions as well as relationships.

If you have fallen into the myth that your mission is your job, you will be trapped when your job description changes, or goes away. Why is it that animals are so willing and wise to migrate when climate changes, or when conditions become unable to support life, yet we humans plant our feet in a factory or a town or a job description even when the source dries up? We may wail and cry but ultimately fail to move on.

Release in Order to Receive

Jesus spoke about another form of release in Matthew chapter 13. Here we meet a wise merchant who sells everything he has to buy the "pearl of great price" (v. 46 KJV). People often focus on this man's getting the great and precious pearl, yet overlook the fact that the merchant took a huge risk to get it—selling everything he had. He had to release the goods he had in order to get the goods he got.

Perhaps you've heard the story of how monkeys are trapped in the wild. The story goes that if you secure a bottle to a tree and put a treat in the bottle, the monkey will reach in, pull it out, and then eat it. Do this a few times, and then put a large banana in there. The monkey will grab the banana, and even after realizing that it can't remove its hand from the bottle, the monkey will still hang on to the banana.

I've been like that, and maybe so have you. We "get a holt" of something, as my sister says, and we can't seem to let it go.

When I realized that if I could release the story I had of myself as a brilliant real estate investor, I might indeed still have a great life. I dropped that banana and went swinging for the forest. My hand hurt for a long time, but at least I was still alive and free.

The gospel teaches us to hold everything lightly, does it not, as this world is passing away?

Make it Yours

List here anything that you think is holding you back because you are holding tightly to it. Title? Position? People? Place?

....

....

One of the characteristics of the Wind personality is that Winds are able to hold things very loosely, picking things up and playing with them a bit, and then releasing them as they swirl on to the next destination. Fires consume, seeing everything as fuel. Waters surround and "pond." Earths see the "gravity" in everything.

Regardless of your elemental makeup, you must be willing to release what you have in order to get the blessing God has for you. Sometimes this is difficult, as the promised blessing is unseen, while the current "benefit" is visible.

Lately my sister, brother, and I have had to endure watching our eighty-eight-year-old mother slowly lose her full vision to macular degeneration. The loss of sight is painful to anyone, but for an artist who seemed to see so much more beauty in the world than others, the loss can be especially painful. As my sister and I were talking about it one day, I told her that I have decided two major things: One is that our mother saw more with her eyes than most people do in a lifetime. She was indeed blessed with "eyes that see." The second is that her sight isn't being "lost"—it is *slowly being transferred, or released,* into the next life that awaits her. I have substituted the sad word *loss* with the happier word *release.* Didn't Jesus teach us the same about life itself?

Jesus said unless a seed falls into the ground, is buried, and "dies," it will never bear fruit. He offered his life as a seed of hope, to be buried and left for dead, so that we could each be released into a new life through him.

Release in Obedient Action

Sometimes God calls us to release our faith in big dramatic actions, like the fiery prophet Elijah. Elijah released great faith, putting his reputation and life on the line in the contest with the prophets of Baal. God honored his faith and released fire as he requested.

My friend Beth Taylor says that God calls us to obey, and then when we do, we get to see the fruit of that, perhaps, and rejoice and relax for a time. But then we are called to a new cycle of faith, and the process seems to start over again. I am amazed at how often I seem to have to learn the same lesson over and over. "Didn't we go over that last year, Lord? Five years ago? Ten years ago? Haven't I progressed at all?"

I've decided that spiritual growth is never linear, but rather takes place in a spiral fashion. So let's say you feel like you are in the exact same spot, having not moved forward at all. But if you were able to see in the multiple dimensions that exist in God's mind, you would see that you are higher up on the loop, having progressed forward in a loop that you cannot see.

Jesus instructed us to release our good works so that all may see them and be blessed. *"Don't hide your light under a bushel"* he admonishes us in Matthew 5:14–16. He also said a candle is not lit and put under a bowl, but is put on a candlestick so that the light may bless all who are in the house.

This is a difficult passage to understand, especially for the Earth and Water personality types who naturally tend to bury their gifts or good deeds. Water, remember, always naturally seeks the lowest place, so asking a Water to stand up and shout,

"I'm over here! I did this good deed! Yoo-hoo!" runs counter to her very personality. However, this passage was made for the Winds and Fires among us. We never saw a bushel basket that couldn't double as a stage. We never saw a little molehill that couldn't be turned into a mountain for conquering.

Of course, I don't think this is what God had in mind—arrogant bragging or calling attention to ourselves. However, it is important to release light wherever you are.

If that light happens to be new information, great. Act on it. If that light happens to be a bold proclamation, act on that, too. The signers of the Declaration of Independence were willing to release their signatures on a document that was ultimately treated as their death warrant by the king of England.

Sometimes we need to sign and send a press release to get some good news out. If you are abiding in Christ and doing what you are called to do, that good news is something that you are a part of, and that is a very good thing. Share it!

Release Your Gifts

A young man named Jonathan can inform and inspire us all with his ability to release. Jonathan is a prototype of Jesus in many ways . . . releasing his throne willingly so someone he loved could have it. Jonathan also seemed to have no heart for ruling but was mostly interested in relationships—with David, his friend, and Saul, his father.

Jonathan "took off the robe he was wearing and gave it to David, along with his tunic, and even his sword, his bow and his belt" (1 Samuel 18:4). He released his earthly title for a greater one. He didn't want to be called "king." He wanted to be called "friend," and like Jesus, he released his royal position so he could be closer to those he loved. He dedicated his life to trying to take care of David, and lost it on the field of battle with his father. He never achieved the worldly power he could have had, but instead sacrificed himself for others.

Release Your Resources

In his book *Negotiating with Giants*, Peter D. Johnston recounts a tale about how a resourceful woman persuaded multiple stakeholders to release their resources for her desired outcome. Listen to how this woman persuaded formerly unconnected people to come together. As is true of many Wind activities, the idea was generated as a friendly game or challenge among friends. Two women were talking, and one said, "I will bet you a bottle of vodka that I can get your son Igor to marry a rich American woman before spring."

The mother of Igor said, "You're on."

So Olga gets busy. She happens to know the owner of one of the largest mining businesses in Russia. She says, "How would you like the son-in-law of a Rockefeller to be on your board?"

He says, "I'd love it." She then sets up a meeting with Rockefeller Sr. through an ambassador, sending a message, "I can get you a board seat on the largest mining company in Russia if you allow me to meet your family."

He does.

She then meets Rockefeller's daughter and says, "How would you like to meet a handsome Russian farmer?"

The daughter says, "You're on."

The daughter meets Igor and falls in love, and they marry. Igor gets a board seat on the largest mining company in Russia and a wife who apparently wanted to get as far away from American business as she could.

Olga wins a bottle of vodka before springtime.

Olga won by identifying the true interests of each party that needed to come together for the transaction to become complete. She also used resources she had at hand. She released her skill set and changed lives in the process.

A variation of this story, which I know happens to be true, had to do with advertising. My sister-in-law works at a large advertising firm in Texas. In its early days the owner of the ad agency had a meeting with Herb Kelleher, CEO of Southwest Airlines, to discuss their account. He said, "How would you like Sea World to agree to your painting some of your airplanes like a giant Shamu to help promote your routes to San Diego?"

Herb asked in awe, "Would they do that?"

The ad-agency owner smiled and said, "Leave it to me."

The ad man then went to SeaWorld and asked for a meeting with the president. He said, "How would you like it if Southwest Airlines agreed to let you paint some of their planes like a giant Shamu to help advertise Sea World?"

The Sea World guy said in awe, "Would they allow us to do that?" The ad man smiled and said, "Leave it to me."

Needless to say, he got both accounts—all by thinking about

how to release the mutual interests of each party into a happy result for all concerned.

Winds are known for their out-of-the-box thinking. With a little bit of extra focus, a Wind personality type is in prime position to see who needs what and who has what other parties need. Winds are the great networkers . . . the great releasers of resources. Waters are great at building in-depth relationships—usually by immersion. Earths, by keeping in mind what needs to grow, can also naturally release their resources. Fires release by flinging themselves deeper and higher into the issue—or they release by running out of fuel on the subject and moving on to another source.

Release Your Wounds

To me, the very essence of Christ is about release. A key principle of Christ is the release of forgiveness. We cannot soar in our careers or in our lives if we hang on to unforgiveness. It is a weight too costly to bear.

At the end of the credits for the TV show *Lost,* there is an animated slice that shows grass in the sunlight, and then you hear the sound of something running. Just as a little square box on legs with a crooked smile rounds the corner, you hear children yelling in unison, "BAD ROBOT!"

This cartoon never fails to tickle me. It is so like us to attribute badness and disobedience to an external force. Did a "bad robot" knock you down? Were you the victim? If you keep putting blame on something else or someone else, you will never heal.

There are many woundings of spirit in the workplace. Yet can we forgive our bosses and coworkers, just as we have been forgiven? If so, we will experience the release of a newly freed heart and soul.

Christ came to release us into abundant life. He came to release us from less than ideal ways of thinking and acting into high performance, high fulfillment, and high satisfaction states of being.

Release Your Inner Leader

"The Spirit of the Sovereign Lord is upon me, because the Lord has anointed me to preach good news to the poor. He has sent me to build up the brokenhearted, to proclaim freedom for the captives and release from darkness for the prisoners" (Isaiah 61:1).

John Walsh, whose six-year-old son was abducted and murdered in 1981, is a courageous example of a man who used his own pain to release resources for other parents whose children were missing, abducted, or murdered. His passion for justice and healing led to a lifetime career of helping the brokenhearted including his hosting the TV program, *America's Most Wanted*. He embraced his wound and became a "wound healer."

How in your career are you helping to set prisoners free? Educators can release people from *ignorance*. Motivational speakers and pastors can liberate those trapped by *fear*, and counselors can help free those imprisoned by *yet-to-be identified issues*.

If and when you identify what you are releasing people from or into, you will be very well received indeed.

I jokingly tell people in my seminars that while Moses, a Water/Fire personality type, kept the Israelites in the wilderness wandering around for forty years, as soon as Joshua, a Wind, got authority, he took them into the Promised Land in *three days*.

When it comes to team building, Jesus ignited, transformed, grounded, and then released his team to do what they had been trained to do. If you are a team leader in your career right now, are you releasing your people, or are you holding them back, micromanaging them into oblivion?

Release Your Gifts

Are you actively releasing your gifts into the world, or are you burying them out of fear?

Jesus did not have kind words for people who did not multiply and release their talents, remember. I tell people that in order to feel fulfilled, you need to be operating in your highest gifts at least 85 percent of the time. This means that you must be in an atmosphere or career choice that allows your gifts to be released.

Jesus also had very strong words for the fig tree that refused to release its fruit. I know many workers who have shut down on the job and yet still show up every day. They will stand there but no way are they going to give any fruit. (No wonder the blind man who had only been touched once by Christ looked around and saw men "as trees walking." He must have been in the marketplace!)

If you are called to teach, have you released yourself to do so? If you are called to speak or preach or sing or write or research or start a business, have you released yourself to do so, or are you still waiting for someone else to give you permission?

I remember speaking in a beautiful opera house in Vienna, Austria. More than 250 people had gathered on a cold winter's night to hear me speak about *Jesus CEO* . . . about how you could be a Christian in business. Afterward, several people came up and gathered around me. Finally, one of them got the courage to speak up.

He said, "Excuse me. We all really want to start a business now. Who do we need to ask to get permission?" My eyes widened at the seeming childishness of the question. Then I realized that I was speaking to people whose parents had been imprisoned in the Nazi army and had the mentality that nothing was done without a dictator's permission. That prisoner mind-set had chained itself around the neck of the next generation, even though they had been free for more than fifty years!

Jesus has already given you permission to release your gifts. Now give it to yourself.

> *I will give you the keys of the kingdom of heaven, whatever you bind on earth will be bound in heaven, and whatever you loose on earth will be loosed in heaven.*
>
> —Matthew 16:19

Jesus, Career Counselor, wants you to *release*, and be released.

CAREER EXERCISES

1. Picture yourself as a gift to the world, all wrapped up in a box with red or blue or yellow ribbon around it. Now picture Jesus eagerly unwrapping the box like a child at Christmas, wanting to get what is inside and hold it up for all to see. Ask a loving friend or family member what it is that could be exciting Jesus about you so much right now. (A good career coach can do the same.)
2. Now picture yourself as a fig tree on a hot and dusty trail. Jesus is looking at you, quite perplexed and angry, because you are not releasing your fruit. What fruit are you supposed to be releasing? I think, deep down in your roots, you know what it is. Name the fruit here:

....

....

3. Now picture yourself releasing the sap it takes to grow the fruit and the abiding joy and blessing that come from releasing the fruit you were designed to share. Picture Jesus happily reaching up and taking the fig from your branches, saying "Ahhh . . . well done, little fig tree. Well done."

4. Who would you be without your excuses? Write your response here:

....

....

....

....

....

A PRAYER FOR YOU

"I can't seem to allow myself to embrace release."

I can't seem to let go . . . of my hurt, my anger, my fears, my petty grievances against others. Help me learn to release the painful past, so I can embrace the healing future. Amen.

CHAPTER TWELVE

REJOICE

rejoice to give joy to: gladden to feel joy or great delight rejoice in: have, possess

I am approaching the train station in northern California. My colleague will pick me up and deliver me to the beautiful headquarters where she and her team work. My heart is starting to quicken, and a smile is spreading across my face because I truly can't wait to see them. I woke up this morning eager to be in their presence again. I do hope I impart wisdom to them, which is what they are paying me for. Yet they give so much to me as well . . . recognition and companionship, a shared sense of mission in this time and place.

I would wish the same for you . . . that you can't wait to be around the people you work with . . . that they recognize and value the gifts within you . . . that they treat you like an honored guest instead of a crazy relative.

Rejoice is a strange word to relate to careers, don't you think? We don't often attribute joy to the workplace—but rather words like *angst* and *sorrow* and *hardship*. Yet God wants us to be joyful in what we do and where we are. Paul said, "Rejoice in the LORD always. I will say it again: Rejoice!" (Philippians 4:4).

Consider Paul in prison, rejoicing at his career surroundings. You have to admit, to the world we Christians can look a little crazy at times. Consider the apostles who entered the Upper Room full of sorrow and mourning, having "lost" their leader in a horrible crucifixion. Next thing they knew, they were emerging with tongues of flames over their heads, speaking in languages they didn't even know they knew. To the world they appeared drunk.

Their careers were about to change, but they didn't know that. They just knew that suddenly they were immersed in joy and power and the presence of their Beloved once again.

Imagine this scenario: You know you are going to die in a matter of days, even though you are young, robust, and healthy. What do you do? Well, Jesus was in that exact position, and you know what he did? He threw a party, to rejoice with those he loved one last time in human form.

> *They left and found things just as Jesus had told them. So they prepared the Passover.*
>
> *When the hour came, Jesus and his apostles reclined at the table. And he said to them, "I have eagerly desired to eat this Passover with you before I suffer. For I tell you, I will not eat it again until it finds fulfillment in the kingdom of God."*
>
> *After taking the cup, he gave thanks and said, "Take this and divide it among you. For I tell you I will not drink again of the fruit of the vine until the kingdom of God comes."*
>
> *And he took bread, gave thanks and broke it, and gave it to them, saying, "This is my body given for you; do this in remembrance of me."*
>
> —Luke 22:13–19

Jesus always advocated throwing a party to rejoice. He was born, literally, during a celestial, special celebration. He spoke of heaven as being a banquet . . . a wedding. Heaven, quite clearly from Jesus' perspective, is all about rejoicing.

Rejoice Through Strife

What if you get a notice that you are laid off? Why not throw a party, invite all your friends, and rejoice? (You would not only shock your friends, but you'd also set a good Christian example, as well as launch your networking outreach immediately.) Who knows what opportunity God is going to show you, now that you can see the potential. Who knows what new people you'll meet, experiences you'll have, things you'll learn. Anticipate it with joy!

Rejoice when the world says cry, and people will wonder what you are up to. "Who do you work for?" they might ask. And you will have a good answer. "Let me tell you who I work for . . . and his ways are not our ways."

Rejoicing Is a Way of Life

Isn't it interesting that the first greeting a human receives when encountered by a heavenly "alien" is not: "You're toast!" or "Gotcha!" Rather, the almost universal message is: "Fear not . . . be happy! In fact, be *very* happy!" God has made the world a joy sandwich, and we are living in the middle of it.

Today I viewed a video of the T-Mobile Dance on YouTube. The telecommunications company hired some dancers to blend into a crowd in a railway station. Suddenly, instead of train announcements, music comes on and people dressed as office workers, youth on the way to school, and business executives break into dance. Amazingly, a number of people surrounding them, caught up in the music, also begin to dance spontaneously. Joy is contagious. And it belongs in the workplace, too.

Are you able to have spontaneous moments of joy in your business or career? Are you rejoicing in the Lord a little bit each day? Yesterday I got off the phone with a CEO I am coaching. He had just had investors visiting his offices for nine days, some from Switzerland, some from Kuwait. The visit went well, as all parties decided to invest what will amount to multiple millions. When I asked him how he handled the stress and energy requirements of hosting so many people at so many levels for so long, he said, "After the last investor left, my staff wanted to get back to work. But I sat down in my office and said, 'Let's pause a moment and savor all of this. We need to rejoice!'"

Rejoicing with Play

We are taught in school the three *Rs* of reading, (w)riting, and 'rythmatic, right? Consider this headline in a recent article written by Tara Parker-Pope: "The 3 R's? A Fourth Is Crucial, Too: Recess"

> *The best way to improve children's performance in the classroom may be to take them out of it.*
>
> *New research suggests that play and down time may be as important to a child's academic experience as reading, science, and math, and that regular recess, fitness, or nature time can influence behavior, concentration, and even grades.*

A study published this month in the journal Pediatrics *studied the links between recess and classroom behavior among about 11,000 children age 8 and 9. Those who had more than 15 minutes of recess a day showed better behavior in class than those who had little or none."*[4]

Play is a time of rejoicing, is it not?

Yet too many of us have forgotten the value of play . . . of celebrating the day . . . of being ecstatic just to be alive. Of giving in to silliness or sharing a good belly laugh with friends.

Make It Yours

When was the last time you "played"? Write it here:

....

What did you do?

....

How do you remember those moments? What is happening to your face, your heart rate, your spirit?

....

....

When can you plan a time for play again, or how can you free yourself up enough to indulge in spontaneous play?

....

....

....

There is a phenomenon called anhedonia, which is the inability to experience joy or pleasure. I think sometimes I have had this disease. I have met other people in the workplace who demonstrated some of the symptoms of the disease I have had. But I hope to combat it. Here's how I came to recognize it . . .

When I was moving a wine rack that I bought to stage one of my houses, I noticed that all of the wine bottles had been emptied and then recorked. I glanced up at the ceiling and noticed what looked like candle smoke rings on what had been newly painted. I shook my head in wonder. "Ah, the skinny-dippers."

It seems the very nice man with a tattoo whom I hired to paint the house while I was out of town took advantage of the situation and threw a party. My next-door neighbor, who also happened to be the listing Realtor at the time, shared with me that one Saturday night he heard loud music, looked over the fence, and saw Chris and crew and family members *en flagratto* splashing away in the pool, with nary a paintbrush in sight.

Only now as I walked through the property, noticing telltale signs of tasks left unfinished, do I realize the extent of how much he and his family enjoyed this house while I was gone. In fact, it is now no wonder to me that a two day paint job lasted three weeks.

They saw it for what it was . . . a party house.

But you know what? I'm not even mad about it. I almost had to laugh. Because they saw something I never saw—not really: that pools are meant to be jumped into, and wine bottles are meant to be opened; that Saturday nights are for partying with the people you work with; and that this house—this wonderful house wanted to . . . was yearning to . . . be enjoyed.

That same night I put my feet into fluffy bath slippers. I had purchased them purely for the intention of putting them by the tub, along with special soaps and bath salts . . . so inviting. I never intended to put my own feet into them. For the last four years I have been staging every house I own . . . setting it up for that imagined potential buyer . . . making each place inviting and alluring and just waiting to be moved into and enjoyed.

Except I never really did enjoy the properties and *live* in them. They were commodities to be bought, remodeled, and sold.

I once laughingly said that I would only buy properties I would live in if something happened to the market, and now it has. Happened. To the market. And I am living in one of my commodities, half as big as my former house, with old windows that need reglazing and a slightly crooked upstairs bedroom floor. The garden wall is in the wrong place, and the floor jobs are Home Depot specials . . . as if someone yelled "Stone on sale" and the former owner just grabbed what he could and laid it down, not matching colors or textures. And yet . . . and yet this house hugs me when I come home. It seems to smile and say, *"Hey, sit down. Take a load off. Put those slippers on. No staging. No preparing for anyone else. Nothing to sell here. Nothing to buy. Welcome home, friend. Welcome home."*

As I write this, I am eyeing a bottle of wine they missed at the party I had unknowingly hosted. The pool looks so inviting . . . I just may slip into it, en flagratto, alive.

* * *

Sometimes, the most creative way to achieve a career-advancement objective is to throw an enormous party. Consider what a little town did in 1917 to attract the attention of shippers who were passing it by on their way to Los Angeles.

I recently learned that Balboa Park was created by the citizens of San Diego in celebration of the opening of the Panama Canal in 1917. The buildings are beautiful, surrounded by reflecting ponds and prados. At one end is a fountain bursting high into the air in front of two museums. What shocked me in reading the history of Balboa Park was that the town of San Diego, at the time of this big celebration's conception, had only thirty thousand people. It was small. It was hurting economically. But somehow the leaders of this town decided that the best way to crack down on "downness" was to have a party and invite the world and dress up the town to do so. Scouting about for an occasion, they hit upon the opening of the Panama Canal, which was taking place, oh, about 2,908 miles away. (Any excuse for a party, right? I have some friends like that.)

Little San Diego held an exposition that took the nation's breath away and put it on the map. Suddenly people up north realized that there were other ports available for delivering their goods. Los Angeles wasn't the only game in town. And in no small part because of this party, San Diego began to grow and prosper, just like the party planners hoped it would.

Rejoice in Dance

One of the things I (and more importantly, God) love about King David is that sometimes he just had to dance. Like the little penguin with happy feet in the animated movie, David's feet would get to tapping. Nevermind his sour-faced wife who felt it was embarrassing or old grumpy men who turned away. David had to dance. He just loved life and God that much. He had happy feet. He knew how to rejoice.

Sometimes it is not enough to praise God with words. Sometimes, we need to give all of ourselves in praise, and it demands that we incorporate our bodies. When did we forget to be free with our movements? When did we become staid and structured and all tied up in our straitjackets?

And when did we forget to celebrate the day and everything in it? "This is the day the LORD has made; let us rejoice and be glad in it" (Psalm 118:24). What does it mean to "be glad" in and out of every meeting and conference call and business lunch?

Deuteronomy 12:18 tells us we "are to *rejoice* before the LORD your God in everything you put your hand to." What this verse is saying is, "If you are going to do it, do it right, do it well, do it joyfully."

Make It Yours

Having trouble figuring out how to rejoice in your everyday life, as God would like you to, today? Here are ten ways to get you started:

1. Eat whatever special treat you never allow yourself.
2. Dance—alone, like nobody's watching, as the saying goes.
3. Sing. Loudly.
4. Make a list of things you're grateful for.
5. Spend time with a child.
6. Take a walk with your best friend.
7. Listen to good music (for a long time).

8. Do an unexpected favor for someone.
9. Send out a thank-you card.
10. Write a love letter to God.

Other Ideas:

Rejoice over Fulfilling Our Promises

When my book *Jesus in Blue Jeans* was finally published, the greater feeling for me was that I had done what I promised God I would do. In many ways, that book will always be my favorite, if only for that reason. I rejoiced over an oath fulfilled.

If we've offered ourselves to our Creator and given all of ourselves to him, even our work, then our work is to be done as something we promised we'd do in his honor. We must remember that we are doing our work as an oath and a prayer to God. We see this in 2 Chronicles 15:15: "All Judah rejoiced about the oath because they had sworn it wholeheartedly. They sought God eagerly, and he was found by them. So the Lord gave them rest on every side."

In all the psalms David wrote, *rejoice* was the most consistent theme of his soul. No wonder God loved him so much! If you look around, you will see all the earth rejoicing at the presence of the Lord. Creation itself sings of his majesty, his amazing work. When told to rebuke his disciples for praising him too loudly, Jesus said, "If they keep quiet, the stones will cry out!"

You know why God created the oceans?

For the whales to play in.

I have goldfish in my pond that deliberately swim through the turbulent part of the water caused by the swirling pump filter . . . as if I've created a water park for them to delight their senses. In their own way, they are rejoicing at being alive in God's creation.

Can you begin to see your workplace as a place to play, to celebrate, to rejoice, rather than a place of drudgery and endless tasks? Might you begin to note how God is present in each coworker and in the work you do?

God says to us, "Rejoice!"

Even some of the grumpiest prophets end up saying, "Rejoice!"

And Jesus, our Career Counselor, wants us to *rejoice.*

> *For you who revere my name, the sun of righteousness will rise with healing in its wings. And you will go out and leap like calves released from the stall.*
>
> —Malachi 4:2

CAREER EXERCISES

1. Where and how are you allowing life to pass you by?

2. Where and why are you constantly "staging things" for others but refusing to rejoice in them yourself?

3. What is this lack of celebration costing you?

4. How often do you laugh at your workplace?

5. How often would you like to?

6. Name twelve reasons you have to celebrate, right now.

7. Have you said thank you to God lately for all of the above?

A PRAYER FOR YOU

"I want to learn how to rejoice,
even when things are difficult."

Dear Lord, I want to learn how to rejoice, even when things are difficult. I want to be able to shout "Yee-haw!" like a cowboy busting out of a gate, with joy and anticipation over the bucking-bronc ride ahead. Turn my whimper into shouts of joy. Please . . . I love you dearly and trust you in all things. I also remember that I was conceived in joy and will be received in joy, so why not rejoice now? Amen.

CREATIVITY AND INNOVATION/WIND BONUS FEATURES

Prayers for Specific Career Concerns

"My kids have left home now, and I am free, but what do I do next?"

Lord, the nest I lovingly made and tended is now empty but for my spouse, the dog, and me. Or maybe only me. I devoted myself fully to raising my family, and I hope and pray I have done a good job. But now I am faced with hours in the day to fill. Perhaps a friend or colleague is calling me, wanting me to come work with her. Will I be up to it? Does she really see who I am? What if I fail? What about those blank spots on my résumé? Help me remember that I have always been fully employed and have been a successful multitasker. That the care and feeding of children is similar to management, and even sometimes harder. Help me realize that the ability to manage and complete projects and the ability to have people with very different ages, personalities, and agendas get along under one roof are skill sets that will serve me in virtually any business of any size in the world.

Help me, like Esther, realize that being a woman "without portfolio" need not keep me from being useful or, indeed, saving a nation. Help me remember that I am not my kids, or my spouse, or even my past. Help me be like the woman at the well, who came to the well feeling thirsty, and left with a bountiful future.

Amen and amen.

"I am caring for my parents and children and working a full-time job. Help!"

Lord, I am stretched multigenerationally. My children have moved back in [or have left their children with me]. My father or mother have no one to properly care for them now. I can joke with my friends that I am changing diapers on eight-month-olds and eighty-year-olds and still making it to work on time. HELP! I feel stretched beyond any elastic in even my fat pants. Are you sure it was a good idea in your plan to have us all live so long? I find myself distracted at work, wondering if everyone at home is okay. Then I get home and can't think of anything but the work piling up on my desk. My e-mails have turned to p-mails as I find myself doing basic chores that I feel so above and overqualified for. And on top of that, I get no thank you. I feel invisible. And exhausted. How many jobs can one person have?

Help me find a boss or a partner who believes in job sharing and flextime. Help me put things in proper perspective so that I have no regrets. And also help me keep my temper in check as others place needs upon me that seem destined to fray my last nerve. You died young on that cross, but even so, you exhorted your friend to take care of your mother. You talked so often of letting the children come to you, too, to be taught and held and encouraged. I try to do all of the above, but, Lord, sometimes I just want to scream, "What about me? What about my needs? My life? My time?" Help me ask for help. Help me set boundaries. Help me take care of myself so I can take care of them. Help me remember, too, that I alone am not responsible for everything. Nor should I be. Be my shepherd, Lord. Lead me to the green pastures, and restore my soul.

Amen and amen.

"I have been laid off, Lord."

For no clear reason that I can understand, my name was placed on a list of people to be released from the company I have been serving faithfully. My mind is reeling with questions: "Why? Why me? Could I have done something differently?" I also admit I am angry at management for getting us in this fix to begin with. If only they were better at their jobs, I might still be employed.

And yet I have placed, and again place, my life in your hands. You see me clearly. You know where I am. You know the talents you have placed within me. I pray and implore you to guide me into my next season of productivity. Where can I be most faithful? Most valued? Most able to contribute my gifts?

If I need to relocate, I am willing. If I need to add to my skill set, I am willing. I do not presume that I gave one hundred percent, every day. I want to, and I recommit myself to, doing all my work as unto you. You are the only Boss I really must please.

You have a new assignment for me, I know you do. Please help me be faithful and diligent in discovering what it is, where it is, and when it shall become evident.

Like a bird searching for the worm, confident that it will find it, I begin my new job search today. I remember that I have wings. I remember that you see me. I remember that your Son said you can count even the hairs on my head.

Help me release my worry and anxiety and anger and begin my search with a renewed heart and mind and soul, knowing you are now, and have always been, my Lord, my Rock, my Salvation. Amen and amen.

Potential Creative and Innovation/Wind Occupations

Every personality type needs to revive, release, and rejoice, but Wind personality types especially will thrive where they are given freedom of expression in industries such as these:

- Communications
- Music
- Restaurant Work
- Tourism
- Sales
- Marketing
- Real Estate
- Entertainment
- Performing Arts
- Politics
- Writing
- Consulting
- Speech Pathology
- Counseling
- Coaching
- Art
- Transportation
- Television
- Health Care
- Education
- Mass Media
- Government
- Faith and Service Organizations

Summary Points

REVIVE: What is your valley of old bones? God is wanting to breathe new life into it—and you.

RELEASE: What are you holding on to that is keeping you from being more productive? Who have you not forgiven?

REJOICE: All of heaven is in a state of rejoicing. When will you join the chorus?

BONUS FEATURES . . .
to Help You Discover Your Life's Work

MY BOOK PICKS

The title: *Get Hired Fast! Tap the Hidden Job Market in 15 Days*
The author: Brian Graham
Published by: Adams Media
Copyright: 2005
Best part: Page 144, "What do you want from your job?"
Tip: Author is a big advocate of direct calling twenty-five friends and fifty companies.

Ninety percent of job openings are unadvertised—learn how to find them.

The title: *The BEST Places to Launch a Career*
The author: Lindsey Gerdes
Published by: BusinessWeek Fast Track/McGraw Hill
Copyright: 2008
Best part: Intensive overview of best places to work, including detailed information from recruiters.
Caution: Many of the places named have since gone under in the accounting, financial, and consulting services categories.

The title: *The Complete Idiot's Guide to Discovering Your Perfect Career*
The author: Rene Carew, Ed.D, with the American Writers and Artists Institute
Published by: Alpha Books/Penguin
Copyright: 2005
Best part: Loads of information on best-paying jobs, least stressful jobs, etc.

The title: *Cool Careers for Dummies*
The author: Marty Nemko, Ph.D.
Published by: Wiley Publishing
Copyright: 2007
Best parts: Guide to affiliate marketing on the Internet; résumé writing; becoming a master communicator.

The title: *202 High-Paying Jobs You Can Land without a College Degree*
The author: Jason R. Rich (note prophetic name)
Published by: Entrepreneur Media
Copyright: 2006
Best parts: How to avoid dead-end jobs; how to make sure you are earning what you're worth; "At a Glance" overview of different jobs including salary potentials, training required, career-advancement opportunities, and job-specific resources per category.

The title: *What Color Is Your Parachute? 2009: A Practical Manual for Job-Hunters and Career-Changers*

The author: Richard Nelson Bolles

Published by: Ten Speed Press

Copyright: 2009

Best parts: Five Worst Ways to Look for a Job; Things School Never Taught Us About Job-Hunting; Value of Passion; Seven Most Important Things to Remember When You Are Unemployed.

Note: Richard Bolles is a former Episcopalian priest who openly discusses his Christian perspective in the book.

The title: *Never Eat Alone: And Other Secrets to Success, One Relationship at a Time*

The authors: Keith Ferrazzi with Tahl Raz

Published by: Doubleday/Random House

Copyright: 2005

Best part: Specific skill sets for networking on the run.

The title: *You Were Made for More*

The authors: Jim Cymbala with Dean Merrill

Published by: Zondervan

Copyright: 2008

Best parts: Analysis of special assignments given biblical characters like Joshua, Gideon, Samson, etc. Heavy emphasis on obedience.

INTERNET RESOURCES

Google.com
CraigsList.org (by city)
Monster.com
TheLadders.com (jobs over $100K)
CareerBuilder.com
Careers.org
EmploymentGuide.com
Federaljobsearch.com (government job search)
Jobing.com
Jobbankusa.com
Summerjobs.com
Usajobs.opm.gov
Hotjobs.yahoo.com
Jobhuntersbible.com
Californiacareers.info
Asktheheadhunter.com
Workblast.com (videorésumés)
OccupationalOutlookHandbook.com
Statejobs.com
eureka.org (Eureka job skills site)

Vault.com (info on careers and individual employers)
Wetfeet.com (same as above)
www.bls.gov/opub/ (Bureau of Labor Statistics Publications)
www.sba.gov (Small Business Administration)
Salary.com
Salaryexpert.com
usnews.com/career (US News Career Center)
www.martynemko.com (five hundred articles)
RileyGuide.com (portal for those trying to choose a career)

WHY RÉSUMÉS SOMETIMES FAIL TO WIN YOU THE JOB

It Takes More

Résumé writing is an art that demands a special skill set. It is also an opportunity for misshaped perceptions and underestimations.

This was an obvious case of a résumé's limitations.

Résumés focus on what you have done, not what you intend to do. They focus on "I did this" lists that you were able to tick off, often under someone else's command. But how does that apply to the true work they, and *you*, are wanting to do?

What if your résumé looked like this.

My name is _____.

1. My mission is to _____, _____, and _____[3 verbs], plus _____[core value] to, for, and with _____[community you wish to influence].
2. My vision is _____.
3. My personality type is _____.

   This means I naturally excel at the following: ________.

4. Here is an example of some things I have been able to accomplish in the past. (Now here comes the traditional résumé.)

Imagine if a job applicant were able to present items one through three before even presenting the résumé? Do you think an employer would be impressed?

We have heard numerous stories of people who got clear about their missions, visions, and personality types' strengths and weaknesses and sat down with employers who often hired them on the spot. One employer said, "You are the most clear and focused person I have ever come across. When can you start?"

You see, your job with the interviewer is to show her you are centered, not off center. You are strong and focused, not needy and compliant. You are aware of the gifts that you bring, and you are eager to offer them.

In fact, many of the people who have answered items one through three never need to write a résumé again, because they know this: once you are clear about what you came here to do, you will never be out of work! You may lose your job, but you will always have work to do. Your task then is to find the next people/site/location who can help you accomplish your mission in the world!

This is the ideal. And it still rings true today, even in this economy.

Here's the catch: *Your mission never involves a job description.* It involves your being able to live out your core value and take actions that align with your personality and calling. For example, I read about a freelance journalist who took a part-time retail job selling clothes, and she is thriving by doing both. Clearly, this person has the mission to communicate and is now happily doing that, both through writing and interacting with customers. She's focused on her mission, not a job description.

So, what's your mission? Look beyond the résumé to where God is leading, follow where he's leading, and you'll find fulfillment on the job front like never before. Because you won't simply find a job—you'll find your *vocation*.

Imagined Interview Scenarios

Scenario 1. You go in with a résumé, sit down silently while the interviewer reads it, then ask if there are any questions. You repeat out loud what you have done in the past, and say you would really like to work there.

Scenario 2. You go in with a résumé, and open with the following: "I am excited to be here today. I know your time is valuable and that you are interviewing several other people, so let me be brief. My mission is to (insert your one sentence mission statement here). My greatest gifts are (insert your four greatest gifts here). My personality type is (insert your personality type here). This means I am really good at (list personality strengths here).

"I've researched your company, and it looks like you need someone who can (list appropriate skill sets here). You also probably need someone who can (list mind-sets here such as Do Systems Thinking, Be Innovative and Creative, Deliver Strategic Planning with Follow Through, Think Globally, Connect the Dots, Energize and Manage a Team)."

For example, my interview might go like this: "My mission is to promote, recognize, and inspire divine connection in myself and others. My greatest gifts are the ability to write, speak, love people, and the freedom to do all of these. My personality type is Wind/Fire, which means I value fast results. My skill sets are Analytical Thinking, Writing Follow Through, Ability to Energize a Team, and to Connect the Dots. Based on my research into your company, it seems to me that you could use someone like me, especially in an industry that is changing so rapidly."

The more clear you are about who you are and what your mission is and your hard-wired skill set, the easier it is for the interviewer to know where you could fit into his or her company and why to hire you!

Don't make them figure it out. Connect the dots for them in an appropriate, respectful, and timely manner.

How to Deal with Sudden Job Loss/ Reversal of Fortune

Perhaps you have been knocked down. The blow came suddenly, without warning, and now you can barely breathe. Your face is on the mat. I know the feeling. It has happened to me, and to millions all around us. Here are some guidelines which might help you.

1. Allow honest grieving. Don't leap immediately into denial or false cheerfulness. Even Jesus wept.
2. Write down your life list of what is really important. Read that list three times a day.
3. Will yourself into faith and rejoicing after proper grieving time. God does have a plan for you larger than you can imagine.
4. Join or rejoin a faith-based community—for encouragement, moral support, job connections.
5. Continue to tithe no matter what. Remember, the widow's oil ended up feeding not only her family but also Elijah the prophet. Let's take a moment to read her story:

The wife of a man from the company of the prophets cried out to Elisha, "Your servant my husband is dead, and you know that he revered the Lord. *But now his creditor is coming to take my two boys as his slaves."*

Elisha replied to her, "How can I help you? Tell me, what do you have in your house?"

"Your servant has nothing there at all," she said, "except a little oil."

Elisha said, "Go around and ask all your neighbors for empty jars. Don't ask for just a few. Then go inside and shut the door behind you and your sons. Pour oil into all the jars, and as each is filled, put it to one side."

She left him and afterward shut the door behind her and her sons. They brought the jars to her and she kept pouring. When all the jars were full, she said to her son, "Bring me another one."

But he replied, "There is not a jar left." Then the oil stopped flowing.

She went and told the man of God, and he said, "Go, sell the oil and pay your debts. You and your sons can live on what is left."

—2 Kings 4:1–7

6. Be resourceful. Sell unwanted, unused items on eBay, CraigsList, or at a yard sale, or donate them.
7. Don't mope. Cope.
8. Seek wise counsel and *professional* help for your transition—hire a life coach, career counselor, transitions counselor. It could be literally a lifesaver for

you. There are people trained and experienced in helping people just like you. Reach out to them. Consider them the life boat when you are drowning in doubt or confusion.

9. Be responsible and seek employment or some new way of generating cash while reducing your expenses.
10. Absorb the idea that retirement does not exist in the animal kingdom, in Scripture, or in the Hebrew language. Working as long as you are able is a healthy way to live.
11. Imagine how your ancestors overcame the difficulties they faced in their times. You represent the strongest and best of your entire lineage so far. Be proud. Be bold. Be confident. "For God did not give us a spirit of timidity, but a spirit of power, of love and of self-discipline" (2 Timothy 1:7).
12. Don't deny yourself the simple pleasures of life either. What activities/pursuits bring you joy? Extract the essence of things you enjoyed—even if you have to do them on a smaller scale.

NOTES

1. Katharine Brooks, *You Majored in What?: Mapping Your Path from Chaos to Career* (New York: Penguin, 2009), 2–5.
2. Maureen Dowd, "The Carla Effect," *New York Times*, June 22, 2008.
3. Dr. Mark Liponis, "You Can Survive Cancer (I Did)," *Parade Magazine*, June 15, 2008.
4. Tara Parker-Pope, "The 3 R's? A Fourth Is Crucial, Too: Recess," *New York Times*, February 23, 2009.

ACKNOWLEDGMENTS

I want to thank John Howard for first approaching me two years ago at a conference and asking, "What have you been thinking about lately?" I want to thank Philis Boultinghouse and Randy Barton, who helped shape my ideas into this manuscript. Philis, you are as strong as you are lovely, gently yet persuasively holding me to a high standard and tight deadline. To Lisa Bergren, thank you for your detailed, thoughtful, and careful edits.

To Jonathan Merkh, what a blessing it is to be with you again in this endeavor.

My colleagues who labor behind the scenes to keep me paddling: Rosario Munoz who handles all things regarding finances, along with Ed Blitz. Lorrie Lievsay does much of the heavy lifting of all things detailed in our organization.

To my mother, Irene Jones, thank you for life itself. To my family, Ben and Kathy, Joe and Barbara, and Bennie and Claudia and Jackson and Reagan, Wade and Janet and Robert Wyatt, your joy and togetherness is a "light that is always on." To my beloved niece Tara with the "auburn" hair; in so many ways my books are written with you in mind.

To the team at America's Christian Credit Union, led by Mendell Thompson, your faithfulness to the values of stewardship and member service is an example of what it is to "reach, serve, and teach." Thank you also to Terri Snyder for handling multiple tasks with ease. Mendell, your "Fire" leadership is the kind that could lead a people out of the wilderness. I find that spending time with you and your team is water for my soul.

To Ken Blanchard, your support and fellowship has been a constant lamp for me. Whether we are splitting a peanut butter sandwich in a hospital room, or sharing lunches at the country club, you and Margie keep me inspired and encouraged. To Phyllis Hendry and Phil Hodges and the Lead Like Jesus team, it is an honor to be working in this field with you.

To Dave Cowan, many thanks to you for helping us design the Path Coaching Program, and doing it with such grace and excellence. Susanna Palomares, your excellence and love of life itself are a constant source of wonder and delight to me.

To my many friends and champions, who are helping people find and live their calling using the material God has given to us, I thank you: Emily Roach, Maria Hall, Nicole Greer, Ruth Adams, Shannel McMillan, Steve Sizemore, Alicia Brown, Allyson Lewis, Ann Starrette, Ashley Hall, Bobbi Stringer, Brenda Staab, Carlin Johnson, Carolyn Nipp, Chloma Ndubuisi, Christine French, Claire Pedrick, Debbie Rose, Deborah Mae Hendricks, Donald Demas, Elise Stanfield, Elizabeth Casanova, Frank Guilano, Georgia Krueger, Helen Park, Jan King, Jeff Stumph, Jim Wideman, John Coyne, Jonamay Lambert, Jud Goldstein, Judy Dean, Julie Driskill, Karen Boyd, Karen Joke, Karen Switzer-Howse, Karl Moeller, Kathryn Sener, Kaylus Horton,

Kim Nance, Kim Polite, Kimber Britner, Kimberly Smith, Lane Henderson, Linda Apple, Lisa Dewar, Maggie Sabatier-Smith, Margi Kyle, Miriam Ezell, Nancy Pennington, Natalie Spitzig, Pam McComb-Podmostko, Patricia Faerber, Patti Tyra, Patty McNally, Peter Walsh, Priscilla Feinberg, Renee Smith, Rhonda York, Robert Cavinder, Ron Harris, Sandra Saylor, Sarah Bailey, Sheila Garner, Sherry McKillop, Simone Monroe, Sonja Corbin, Susan Naylor, and Teresa Kilpatrick.

To the organizations that have so kindly invited me to share my thoughts and work with them, I also offer gratitude.

To George Barna, thank you for including me in your *Masters of Leadership* book. It was an honor to be considered among such fine company.

To Beth Taylor and her husband, Paul, thank you for converting your home into our Dallas headquarters. If every meeting around the world could be held in your bistro/wine cellar, the world would be a happier and more productive place.

To Lisa Rose and the amazing First Friday team, thank you for hearing and then implementing such a creative plan. I always told people Jesus loves going to the movies, and when you put me in Harkins theater, it was a surprise to actually be the movie everyone came to see.

To Cozy Dixon and her husband, Pastor Steve, you are always there for me when I need you. Thank you for being the love of Jesus wherever you go. For Vickie Ward, who has brought new life and vigor to our Path for Children program, may you receive tenfold the blessings that you bring.

To Sonja Brown, for excellent research on the scriptures pertaining to the twelve chapter headings. To Jacque Salamy, who provided clues, as needed, about which career picks might match chapter headings. To Elisa Hulston, who serves her students faithfully; to Virginia Arteaga, who handles diplomatic issues with ease in three languages; to Major Bill Collins, who serves as adviser to the Speaker of the House on veterans' affairs; and to Dick Stenbakken, whose laughter and faithfulness always show up at just the right time.

Shelly Buckner, a person who has the amazing ability to work out of both sides of her brain while still engaging her heart, is a constant example to me of someone who pours herself fully into all she does. Shelly, you help me grow and thrive as you daily live your mission. To Catherine C. Calhoun, my friend and mentor, thank you for river walks and long phone talks and listening to me in a way that goes deep into my soul. You have been a never-ending source of wonder, support, and life to me.

To Jesus, who plays with me, sings to me, flirts with me, sends me little love messages throughout the day, where would I be without you? Help me show them, Lord, what it is like to be held in your arms. To experience the joy that comes from knowing unconditional love. To experience the ever-growing goodness and expansion of life in you. Help me help them to fully live their dreams.

And to you, the reader, thank you for taking the time to rise and risk and roar with me. To spend these hours together as we reflect, renew, and restore. I pray that these words will help you remain, return, and regenerate. And may you also and always revive, release, and rejoice. Such is our lot in life: to know and be known by our Creator, who sings over us with joy.

OPPORTUNITIES TO LEARN MORE FROM LAURIE BETH JONES

www.lauriebethjones.com

Finding Your Path experience, training, and licensing

Path for Teens training and licensing

Path for Kids licensing

Path Coach Training and certification

Path Elements Profile (PEP) training, licensing, and certification

Business Growth and Development through individual/group consulting

Keynote speeches

Graduation speeches

Board retreats

Other books written by Laurie Beth Jones

Jesus, CEO: Using Ancient Wisdom for Visionary Leadership

The Path: Creating Your Mission Statement for Work and for Life

Jesus in Blue Jeans: A Practial Guide to Everyday Spirituality

The Power of Positive Prophecy: Finding the Hidden Potential in Everyday Life

Grow Something Besides Old: Seeds for a Joyful Life

Jesus, Entrepeneur: Using Ancient Wisdom to Launch and Live Your Dreams

Teach Your Team to Fish: Using Ancient Wisdom for Inspired Teamwork

Jesus, Life Coach: Learn from the Best

Personal Notes to the Graduate: 24 Values to Shape Your Destiny

The Four Elements of Success: A Simple Personality Profile that Will Transform Your Team

We currently have trained consultants in the United States, United Kingdom, Canada, South Africa, and New Zealand. More countries will be added.

If you would like to become a trainer or for more information, please go to our website at www.lauriebethjones.com.

EXPLORE THE VISION GOD HAS FOR YOU

Use the space in these last few pages to make whatever notes you wish to help you discover God's dream for you . . .

Printed in the United States
By Bookmasters